"BRAIN DRAIN" FROM RUSSIA: PROBLEMS, PROSPECTS, WAYS OF REGULATION

"BRAIN DRAIN" FROM RUSSIA: PROBLEMS, PROSPECTS, WAYS OF REGULATION

Stanislav Simanovsky
Margarita P. Strepetova
Yuriy G. Naido

NOVA SCIENCE Publishers, Inc.
New York

Art Director: Maria Ester Hawrys
Assistant Director: Elenor Kallberg
Graphics: Denise Dieterich and Maryann Miglorino
Manuscript Coordinator: Roseann Pena
Book Production: Tammy Sauter, and Benjamin Fung
Circulation: Irene Kwartiroff and Annette Hellinger

Library of Congress Cataloging-in-Publication Data

Simanovskiĭ, s.
    Brain drain from Russia: problems, prospects, and
regulation/ S. Simanovsky, M.P. Strepetova, Yu. G. Naido.
        p. cm.
    Includes bibliographical references and index.
    ISBN 1-56072-263-0 :
    1. Brain drain--Russia (Federation) 2. Brain drain --
Former Soviet republics. 3. Brain drain--Europe, Eastern. I.
Strepetova, M.P. (Margarita Petrovna) II. Naido, Yu. G.
(Yuriy G.) III. Title.
    JV8190.S56 1996   95-25322
    304.8'.0947--dc20   CIP

© *1996 Nova Science Publishers, Inc.*
    6080 Jericho Turnpike, Suite 207
    Commack, New York 11725
    Tele. 516-499-3103 Fax 516-499-3146
    E Mail Novasci1@aol.com

Printed in the United States of America

CONTENTS

PREFACE

"Brain drain" - intellectual emigration - exodus of the elite of the society which to a considerable extent defines its cultural, scientific, technological and socio-economic progress and its contribution to the global civilization takes a growing international scale.

For many decades "brain drain" was substantially unknown to the former Soviet Union and existed as a thin stream in a relatively weak current of ethnic emigration (mainly Jewish, German, Greek, Spanish). Emigration itself was either ignored or regarded by the society as a phenomenon incompatible with the socialist system or even as high treason. Hence the humiliating procedures to which persons who decided to emigrate were subjected both by the state authorities and the public at large; they insulted human dignity and violated human rights and freedoms.

So, "brain drain" was confined previously to countries of the so-called "non-socialist world", mainly to developed industrial states of the West as a consequence of the Second World War. Thus, between 1949 and 1965 about 97,000 high-skill scholars emigrated to the USA, mainly from Great Britain, Germany and Canada. Since the mid-1960's and in particular during the 1970's the geographic structure of the "brain drain" process noticeably changed, the developing countries becoming its "nutrient medium". During 1961-1980 more than 500,000 specialists (mainly scholars, engineers, medical personnel) from developing countries moved to the USA, Great Britain and Canada. [1].

With the decomposition of the "world socialist system" and the breakup of the USSR the "brain drain" is taking the character of one of the most important global problems of present days. As regards its scale and dynamism, the present-day and expected intellectual emigration from countries of Eastern Europe and the former USSR substantially exceeds the previous processes in this sphere and starts to noticeably affect the international migration flows, their character, intensity and structure, and, hence, the world demographic, socio-economic and political situation.

Since the beginning of the 1990's emigration from the former Soviet Union takes a snow-slide character. Many people, including scientists and specialists, having exclaimed like Alexander Pushkin, a world-famous Russian poet of the 19-th century, "And what for I, with my brains and talent, was born in Russia?" rushed to leave their homeland in search of a better use of their capabilities, more decent conditions of work and existence.

Since the beginning of the 1970's more than 1 mln. people left the country, including over 600,000 during the last three years. Only in 1990 the number of emigrants from the USSR was the following: to Israel - 267,000 persons, to Germany - 142,000; to the USA - about 70,000. The number of scholars and specialist with higher education among those emigrants was approximately 100,000 persons. According to some estimates available at that time, with the enforcement of the USSR Law (enacted in 1991) on Immigration and Emigration in 1993, 8-10 mln. people could leave the countries of the newly formed (instead of the former USSR) Commonwealth of Independent States (CIS) by the end of the 1990's at an annual average figure of potential emigrants of 1-1.5 mln. persons with the number of representatives of the intellectual elite in this flow reaching 200,000-250,000 persons. [2].

However, the alarming forecasts of some home and foreign experts about an avalanche-like emigration (i.e. departure from the homeland for a permanent residence abroad) from the former USSR did not come true, actual figures are more modest - at least 3-4 times lower, as it is shown in respective chapters of the book. Nevertheless, taking into consideration great numbers of migrants (i.e. those leaving home country for a temporary stay abroad), this process of a mass exodus is detrimental, since it means a full (permanent or temporary) exclusion of a sizeable part of the country's human potential from its use in the national economy.

The greatest actual and potential damage to the national economy of Russia and other countries of the CIS is due to the mass exodus of researchers, professors and lecturers, engineers and technicians. According to calculations of UN experts, emigration of one specialist of this category causes a damage of about $300,000 to his country. At an average minimum proportion of these intellectuals of 5-10% of the total number of emigrants, this means that emigration

of scholars and engineers might bring an annual potential loss of
$2.5-5 bln. to Russia only.

In addition to direct and implicit losses, "brain drain" can exert
a negative effect on scientific and technological development of the
country, its intellectual and cultural level, thus widening the gap between East and West and decelerating the progress of economic reforms and of the socio-economic development of the nation in general.

In the book the "brain drain" process is considered as consisting
of two components: ethnical emigration and labour migration which
are interconnected in a dynamic equilibrium.

Prevailing until recently was the first component - emigration of
scientists and other intellectuals for the reasons of mostly ethnic
character. These are the consequences of the previous "Leninist" national policy now taking the form of bloodshed ethnic conflicts, dis-
crimination law and practices of authorities in respect of ethnic minorities; these are also the return to historical homeland and reunification of families.

For the emigrants of this flow, in contrast to labour migrants, the
mere economic factors are not decisive. The restoration of national
dignity, elimination of the feeling of being a second-sort citizen, liquidation of the inferiority complex, faith into a better future for
themselves and their children frequently become the "last straw"
factors defining the final solution for emigration, sometimes to the
detriment of considerations of well-being.

For the CIS countries this ethnic component of "brain drain" is a
mere waste, an irreversible (and in many cases hardly compensated) loss of the intellectual potential of culture, science and production. In the short- and medium-term perspective this flow is not
susceptible of limitation or even control. This requires a radical
change of the entire political and socio-economic situation inside the
country, a respective revision of ethnic policy principles, and of the
general role of culture and science in the society, the place of intellectuals in the societal progress, provision of decent conditions for
labour and homelife matching those of a civilized state.

Though a respective mechanism of state policy in this sphere
should be designed already now, it will give tangible results only in
a distant future. At the present stage one can expect only a further
intensification of the ethnic component of "brain drain" which will
be promoted also by a growing democratization of Russian society,
a greater extent of its openness to the external world, adherence to

a true observation of international norms regarding human rights, in particular the right for choice of the place of residence and work.

The second component of "brain drain" - labour migration - is an outflow of scientists and specialists for a temporary (though, possibly, rather long-lasting) work on a contract and on their personal initiative of a free search for a suitable application of their creativity and for normal living conditions. In this case the decision for a labour migration out of the home country is dictated mainly by economic factors.

The present political and socio-economic situation gives all reasons to think that labour migration from Russia and other CIS countries abroad will soon become, as to its scale and dynamics, the leading component of the general "brain drain" process, even exceeding the ethnic migration.

The labour migration, as a component of the "brain drain" process, nevertheless, is even now susceptible of institutional, legal and socio-economic control on both national and international levels, although a certain portion (up to 15% according to some estimates) of this flow may become an irreversible loss for the home country, since some scholars and specialists (especially younger ones) for some personal reasons might prefer to stay in host countries for permanent residence.

The notion "irreversible loss" in both components of the "brain drain" process is quite conditional. The intellectual migration is a reflection of objective processes of internationalization of economic life, of growing interdependence of countries and regions of the world, so that the migrants who left their home country forever or for some time make, nevertheless, their contribution to the progress of the world science and technology, to the benefit of the global civilization and, through international economic and scientific-and-technological cooperation, this contribution finds its use in the national economy of their home country as well.

Thus, the "brain drain" process combines three groups of interests: personal interests of its individual participants who, as a rule, gain from changing their citizenship or residence, national interests of home and host countries losing or gaining respectively from "brain drain", and interests of the international community that never loses and only gains from such human exchanges. Hence, two main conclusions follow from this situation.

First, all the three groups of interests should be harmonized, so that the state-national interests of the losing donor countries be compensated in some way. This justifies to a great extent their right for taking protective measures to make the possible damage minimal, as well as their right for a certain reimbursement of the actual losses both from the gaining recipient countries and the world community as a whole.

Second, to find a reasonable compromise mutually acceptable and satisfying interests of all the three groups of participants of the "brain drain" process, the latter should be regulated on the international level by way of appropriate bilateral agreements between home and host countries concerned, or multilateral agreements, also within the framework of international organizations.

These considerations define the contents of the book which includes respective chapters dealing with socio-economic implications of "brain drain", methodology of determination of "waste" and "gain" effects for donor and recipient countries, the present state and prospects of international cooperation in coping with the problem of "brain drain" from Russia and other countries of the CIS. The intellectual emigration from these countries is analyzed in the book as a part of the global "brain drain" process catalyzed during recent years by intellectual exodus from countries of Central and Eastern Europe (CEE) which together with the former Soviet Union are now in the epicenter of the current migration boom.

"Brain drain" is treated in the book as a global international problem on the basis of a hypothesis stemming from the logic of the concept disclosed by John K. Galbraith, a world-known American economist in his fundamental treatise "The New Industrial State" (Mifflin Publishing House, Boston, 1967). He put forward the idea, supported by convincing arguments, of a consecutive historical gaining of economic and political power first by feudals (landlords), then by capitalists and, finally, by technocrats.

Their coming to power was the result of struggle for the key objects of ownership in every successive historical stage: land, capital, technologies. Such struggle took place on both national and international levels. In the latter case it was accompanied first by a territorial division of the world (this process is already substantially completed), then by the global division of capitals and technological markets (this process is still ongoing). As regards the global "brain drain" process, it is, in the authors' opinion, a new form of a next, more profound, redevision of the world intellectual resources. If this assumption is true, further development of the process will be inevitably accompanied by a stronger international competition for creators of scientific knowledge and high technologies - i.e. by the struggle for "brains". In other words, he who has "brains", rules the world.

Would this struggle result in a further strengthening of international positions of the already shaped technological centers of the world (USA, Japan, Western Europe), or other states would be able to wedge in their ranks; what is the role of Russia in this process, could it become the fourth high-tech world center - only time can give final answers to these and many other related questions. But it is quite clear now that an active involvement of Russia and other post-socialist states in the global "brain drain" process means the beginning of the decisive stage of intellectual redivision of the world, the outcome of which is likely to be seen in the next century. The world community should be ready to such course of developments and prepare an adequate response to it.

The "brain drain" problem has been recently debated in international mass media mainly in connection with an exaggerated opportunity of a mass-scale exodus of nuclear scientist and engineers from the former Soviet Union and the appearance of nuclear and other military (chemical, biological) technologies in hot spots of regional conflicts, other places of tension and confrontation, and in the hands of international terrorists.

Known are numerous cases of recruitment of nuclear scientists and specialists from the USSR, mainly from Russia, by foreign countries. Thus, ten researchers signed contracts with Algeria, four specialists offered their services to India; 50 specialists are in Iraq. Since 1992 14 nuclear engineers stayed in Iran which in 1993 employed additional 50 engineers and 200 technicians from the CIS countries for a salary of $5,000 a month for assembling nuclear warheads. Libya signed contracts with several former researchers of Moscow Kurchatov Nuclear Institute for work on Sydra-Bay project for a salary of $100,000 a year. In Israel about 60 former Soviet citizens are working in nuclear engineering area.

Russian nuclear "brains" go not only to the West, but to the East and South as well. About 160 ex-Soviet specialists helped North Korea to create its own nuclear bomb. In December 1992 Russian authorities detained in Moscow airport 36 nuclear scientists going to North Korea to work at its nuclear facilities. South Korea invited 300 Russian specialists from defense industries. Even in Taiwan more than 30 ex-Soviet defense industry employees, including 12 from Russia and 10 from the Ukraine, found jobs on their professions. [3].

In countries of the former USSR there are altogether about 3,000 nuclear scientists and 5,000 specialists in the manufacture of fission materials [4] (according to William Potter, Director of the Center of Russian and Soviet Studies, Institute of International Studies, Monterey, California, USA, their total number is about 10,000 persons [5]) who are potentially ready to emigrate due to the ill-considered and improperly realized policy of conversion of the defense sector, the cease of the demand for their knowledge and experience, and the worsening conditions of their life in the home country.

In view of this situation the international community became anxious . The NATO Secretary General M.Werner said that "brain drain" in the area of nuclear technologies is more dangerous than propagation of nuclear weapons themselves, since it is substantially uncontrollable. [6]. Prof.N.Naimark, Director of the Center for Russian and East-European Studies, Stanford University, USA, noted: "It is quite clear that if nuclear specialists do not lose their job in Russia, Ukraine or Kazakhstan, this will be the best solution for all of us".[7].

Western countries began searching appropriate measures to prevent the undesirable emigration and migration of nuclear (and other military) technology specialists from Russia and other countries of the former USSR.

Respective chapters of the present book provide a detailed disclosure of the scale and forms of activities of the West in respect of the ongoing and expected intellectual emigration from the former Soviet Union, their efforts to regulate this "brain drain" on the national, bilateral and multilateral levels.

These measures relate to the introduction of more severe provisions in national immigration laws, quotas and contingent restrictions for the flows of immigrants, tighter age and professional requirements, medical conditions, as well as other provisions (e.g. high costs of making necessary visa formalities) limiting the total flow of immigrants.

On the other hand, national legislation regulating immigration of high-skill scientific and technological personnel are revised towards granting additional preferences, rights and opportunities for a better integration of intellectual immigrants into the scientific community of the receiving countries.

Thirdly, measures have been taken to keep the scientific and technological human potential directly in the countries of a potential exodus, i.e. at home, by way of retention of the existing and creation of new jobs, by elaboration of bilateral and multilateral programmes and projects for domestic absorption and adjustment of scientists and specialists released as a result of restructuring of the national economy, of conversion of the defense industries, by financial support of international cooperation and contacts of scientists and engineers from Russia and other CIS countries with their foreign colleagues, etc.

This seems to be the most important direction of both individual and concerted efforts of Western countries in regulation of the process of "brain drain" from the former USSR, since it provides an opportunity of a direct positive influence on the reasons, motives and factors underlying it, i.e., in general, on the present state and prospects of national science and technology.

The analysis of Russia's R&D sphere is given in the book against a general background of the current tense socio-economic situation in this country, so as to enable the reader to get a better understanding of the motivations and reasons (which are also described in the book in detail) enhancing emigration moods of Russian people, researchers and engineers in particular.

The book also suggests the measures that Russia has to take itself and in cooperation with foreign countries so as to improve the present situation in its science and technology, eliminate the negative factors pushing intellectuals out of their own country, make their international contacts, either at home, or through labour migration abroad, beneficial for themselves and their homeland.

These measures are to be implemented within the framework of a strategy based not on the principle of diminution of the emigration flow (which, in fact, would mean restrictive and prohibitive steps, i.e. return to the former totalitarian system and violation of human rights and freedoms), but on the principle of minimization of losses brought by "brain drain" to Russia's national economy, by way of a further democratization of Russian society, positive socio-economic transformations in its transition towards a market economy.

The authors hope that this book will be of interest to scholars and analysts, experts and professionals in science and innovation policies, demography and migration, economics and political sciences, as well as to all those who want to know what is going on in the modern Russia and in its relations with the international community on the way of reintegration into the global civilization.

REFERENCES

1. "Osteuropa Wirtschaft", 1/94, p.17.
2. Ibid., p.18.
3. "Herald of the Russian Academy of Sciences", 1993, vol.63, No.9, p.649; "The Moscow Tribune", January 14, 1993, p.12; "Izvestiya", 27.01.94, "Rossijskiye Vesti", 16.02.94.
4. "Osteuropa Wirtschaft", 1/94, p.20.
5. ITAR-TASS, 03.02.92, COMPAS No.21,p.6.
6. "Brain Drain" from Russia: Problems, Prospects, Ways of Regulation. Report to UNESCO-ROSTE Seminar, February 21-23, 1994, p.17.
7. ITAR-TASS, op.cit.,p.5.

Chapter I

BRAIN DRAIN" - GLOBAL PROBLEM OF THE PRESENT-DAY WORLD

1.1. MOBILITY OF POPULATION AND ORIGINATION OF "BRAIN DRAIN" PHENOMENON

Mobility of population dates back to ancient times. Our ancestors whose main activity was hunting and animal breeding were "doomed" to a nomadic way of life. And though migration took place mainly in groups, in a tribe community individual inter-tribe contacts occurred, mixed families and more stable inter-tribal congregations originated for solving some common problems and later they developed on a continuous basis. It can be assumed that even in those times the most active and clever members of such human associations (a sort of "intellectual elite") became initiators of contacts. The shift to a settled way of life, progress of handicrafts, arts and culture in general, appearance of farms and large manufacturing shops put an end to global migration flows the peak of which were "great people movements". However, this did not mean ceasing of migration flows in general: mobility of population took other forms due to changes in its motivation. There appeared a specific demand in the society for skilled craftsmen, healers, architects and construction workers, experienced warriors, poets and artists, as well as for a non-skilled labour force the need in which was satisfied by capturing into slavery, forced recruitment, expelling from lands, etc.

The great geographic discoveries revived migration flows, mobility of the "stale" society by the end of the medieval period noticeably increased. Nevertheless, a relatively underdeveloped maritime and ground transportation system was a serious obstacle for the inter-state migration, especially in the absence of common borders.

Analysis of migration flows on a time scale makes it possible to note, in them, a gradual shaping of the phenomenon which later was named "mobility of intellectual labour". Pheudal landlords and kings widely practiced leasing of various craftsmen, frequently resorting to violence methods. Here we already see the outset of the phenomenon of "brain drain". Either time, migration, "brain drain" including, in a number of countries becomes a constituent of a governmental policy and exerts a noticeable influence on the socio-economic situation (for example, in the USA, Russia, Mexico, Israel, India, Pakistan, Middle East countries, etc.).

"Brain drain" as an international problem in its modern interpretation originated in the post-war period. The winner countries entering a new stage of scientific and technological development felt an acute deficit of high-qualification specialists and initiated finding ways of solving this problem. The United States and the Soviet Union were first to invite talents from abroad. For example, 4-5 thousands of German specialists in rocket engineering and other advanced areas were taken to the USA.[1]. Many German scientists and engineers also took part in implementation of Soviet missile program after completion of which some of them returned home, mainly to East Germany. The attraction of foreign specialists becomes an intentional governmental policy which is then corrected by individual states, groups of states depending on the changing situation in the world. Immigration laws are adopted which define a system of measures encouraging attraction of high-skill labour force and legalizing position of the newcomers in the host countries.

During the period after the WWII till the end of the 80's it is possible to single out two basic migration flows characterized by a high proportion of intellectuals in them. [2]. During the 50's these flows concentrated mainly in the developed countries and the main center of their destination were the United States of America. The flows originated mostly in Great Britain and Canada. It is likely that the term "brain drain" itself was invented and introduced into the literature by Britishers.

During the 70's the flow of high-skill personnel from Western Europe to the United States gets noticeably declined. Great Britain, Canada and West Germany cease to be the main donor countries. Their share in the total immigration flow of specialists to the USA is sharply reduced: that of Great Britain in 1972 - to 2.7%, of Canada - 1.5%, West Germany - 1.1%. [3].

The geographic structure of "brain drain" is also changed. The North-South scheme starts to act in the second stage of the development of international migration. During the 70's the developing countries took the dominating role in this process and their share in this period was as high as 70-80% (vs. 33% in 1956). [4].

The United States managed to keep and, in this stage, even to take the leading role in attraction of specialists from the total flow of high-qualification emigrants. During the 60's and 70's "brain drain" from developing countries to the USA was 61% on the average, to Canada - 26% and to Great Britain - 22%. [5]. Thus, while during 1966-1978 about 188,000 high-skill specialists altogether emigrated to the USA, nearly 115,000 out of them were from developing countries. The greatest number of qualified personnel immigrated to the USA during this period originated from Asia - about 60 thousands of researchers and engineers, 10.3 thousands - from Latin America countries, 4,700 specialists - from Africa. [6].Great Britain and Canada became major immigration centers. Thus, nearly half the number of immigrants in Great Britain - teachers, doctors, engineers and researchers were former citizens of developing countries; in Canada the proportion of the third world citizens in the general inflow of immigrants was even higher. [7].

During 1961-1980 more than 500,000 qualified specialists of various professions emigrated to the USA, Great Britain and Canada from developing countries.

During the 80's a new phenomenon is observed - origination of immigration flows between developing countries themselves. Several crisis waves ensured a great income growth for a number of developing states and promoted not only the development of oil-extracting and oil-refining industries, but a general progress of their economies as well. Lack or shortage of local personnel necessitated a mass-scale import of high-skill labour force, including from developing countries. In 1980 about 20,000-25,000 specialists from Egypt, Jordan, Yemen, India, Pakistan, Turkey worked in such Arab countries as Libya, Saudi Arabia, Bahrain, Kuwait, United Arab Emirates, etc. The share of specialists in the general flow of immigrants increased and reached more than half their total number by the mid-80's (55.9% in 1985).

A specific feature of migration between Arab states is that it occurs within the framework of a single cultural area where between the migrants and the local population there are substantially no differences in the language, religion, socio-cultural values. This factor to a great extent smoothes some negative aspects of international migration, removes tension between the migrants and the local population. The deepening of the economic differentiation between developing states will apparently promote expansion of migration flows inside the third world. This is also facilitated by the growing competition in respect of immigration, to the USA and Western Europe, from countries of the former Soviet Union and Eastern Europe.

The term "mobility of scientists and engineers" has but a limited application to the past and present realities of the former USSR countries. The centrally planned system of economic management excluded free market in general, and market of labour force in particular. Training and distribution of scientists, engineers, doctors, teachers, etc. was effected all-over the country on a plan basis. The only exceptions were so-called competitions (contests) for filling vacancies at various educational and research institutions, joining post-graduate and doctorate courses, so-called "organized recruitment" of intellectual manpower for strengthening R&D, technological and production potential of underdeveloped remote regions of Russian North, Far East, Siberia and national republics of the former Soviet Union. These flows defined the pattern (both geographic and specialization in science disciplines) of so-called "mobility" of scientists and engineers.

The situation was aggravated also by lack of market of lodging facilities, by the system of residence permit ("propiska" in Russian, or an obligatory assignment to a certain location without right to live in any other area). Such was the internal mobility in the former USSR. It had no explicit reflection in the state statistics whatsoever and could be estimated only by sophisticated calculations and expert assessments.

Now, with the breakup of the former Soviet Union, further development of democracy, declared adherence to human rights and common human values, gradual transition towards a market-type economy, appearance of different types of ownership and of various components of the national market such as markets of labour force, dwelling facilities, development of a social infrastructure, a new additional positive impetus will be given to migration of scientists and engineers within Russia and other countries of the former USSR, so that the term "mobility" will acquire its full meaning.

However, the process of mobility of scientists and engineers in Russia and other CIS countries occurs now against a negative background of a worsening situation in Russian R&D sphere in general, conversion of the military-industrial complex and a related release of high-skill labour force overflowing to other spheres of the national economy and to other geographic regions thus creating a very tense socio-economic situation pregnant with a blast of unemployment. This is aggravated by territorial disputes in some regions of Russia and other former Union republics, interethnic conflicts resulting in a mass-scale exodus of Russian-speaking intellectuals from these areas to Russia where they can only complicate the situation in the market of intellectual labour force and cause additional social tension. This necessitates elaboration of a comprehensive programme of their absorption and adjustment in the Russian society.

On the other hand, the former Soviet Union was a closed society so that mobility of scientists and engineers abroad was also of a limited character. It was confined mainly within the socialist countries of Eastern Europe, Asia and Cuba where Soviet intellectuals were sent on special missions for the formation and strengthening of national R&D potentials of these countries. Soviet scientists and specialists worked at international coordination centers, international research institutes, laboratories and other socialist international organizations, delivered lectures at educational institutes, vocational training centers, practiced in hospitals and other medical institutions.

Many students and post-graduates from these countries studied at Soviet universities and institutes, scholars obtained their academic degrees in Soviet research institutes and international R&D centers located in the USSR territory. This (also planned) mobility was a two-way street with rather intensive traffic which was regulated on both bilateral and multilateral (COMECON) level. It reached its climax by the mid-80's (when a Comprehensive Programme of Scientific and Technological Progress of the COMECON Member Countries up to the Year 2000" was adopted) and in many cases it was of a productive character and exerted a positive effect on the development of R&D and production potentials of the countries of the former "socialist community".

Since the late 80's (1987-1989) this mobility began to decline and reduced to a minimum (on the official level) with the collapse of the "world socialist system". Now it exists on a limited scale as a part of a general labour-migration process, in many cases semilegal or illegal, one-way oriented ("from Russia with love") and focused mainly on such countries as Poland, Czechia, Hungary.

As regards industrially developed countries of the West, mobility of Soviet scientists and engineers was limited mainly to participation in international or national conferences, symposia and other scholarly events, student-exchange, post-graduate and doctorate programs, lecturing at foreign universities as visiting professors, training at university and plant laboratories, as well as at production facilities of various foreign companies when purchases of foreign equipment and technologies were made by the Soviet Union and respective contracts envisaged training of Soviet personnel at foreign enterprises. A certain number of specialists also worked in international organizations where they were replaced by other Soviet citizens on expiration of their contracts.

Many Soviet scientists, engineers, medical personnel and other specialists worked and still are working in developing countries, mainly as university professors, field engineers in extraction of natural resources, construction engineers, doctors at hospitals and clinics, instructors at vocational training centers, pilots at local airlines, instructors for operation of Soviet-made weapons, engineers and technicians at service and maintenance locations intended for servicing the Soviet-made equipment delivered to developing states.

This mobility of scientists and engineers from the former Soviet Union to the West and the third world was also effected in a planned manner regulated by intergovernmental agreements, not by personal contracts of individuals, because no legislation stipulating free-will migration of Soviet intellectuals abroad existed at that time. Out of the total number of scientists and engineers from the former Soviet Union involved in this process of external mobility about 65-70% were concentrated in ex-socialist countries, 15-20% - in developing states, and the remaining - in industrially developed countries of the West.

With the collapse of the world socialist system and breakup of the former Soviet Union all these mobility processes lost their plan-regulated character, since their legal framework disappeared, and took on the form of ethnic emigration and labour migration both within the territory of the former Soviet Union and abroad.

A new boom of migration processes in the world is observed during late-80's - early-90's as a result of growth of industry, development of transport and communication systems, acceleration of general scientific and technological progress. The recent studies show that investment into "human capital" in many industries become comparable with expenses for the basic and circulation production capital. This trend will inevitably exert a strong impact on expansion of migration of scientific and technical personnel. That is why governments of many countries continue to follow a persistent purposeful policy for attracting the most qualified manpower and specialists with the view to saving costs and speeding-up innovation.

Realization of such policy is possible owing to a relatively high mobility of intellectuals. A high mobility of scholars, engineers, specialists and creative workers in other areas of human knowledge is, in turn, defined by a supra-national, non-state nature of knowledge, culture and art in the modern society. Enhancement of economic interdependence and mutual complementation in the formation of global economy give new a impetus to interstate migration of scientific-and-technical intelligentsia. At the present time the "foreign contribution" of the intellectual elite to the progress of human civilization is so great that it can be regarded as a new phenomenon combined with a similar activity within national-and-state borders.

The trans-border character of many economic processes, numerous international intergovernmental and public organizations along with a well-developed international communication system have created a sound legal and material basis for an unprecedented intensification of migration flows, extended the possibilities of scholars and specialists to utilize their creative potential not only in their home country, but in foreign countries as well.

To understand the scale and character of migration flows of scientists, specialists and creative individuals, it is necessary to analyze motivation, factors and reasons moving them abroad and joining the ranks of intellectual migrants.

1.2. MOTIVES, REASONS AND FACTORS OF INTELLECTUAL MIGRATION

First of all, it should be noted that the "human factor" plays a growing role in the modern society in general and in its economic life in particular. A severe competition between manufacturers, increasing requirements of consumers spoilt by supremacy of the supply over the demand make producers continuously renovate their products, improve technologies, enlarge the range of goods and services. The ability of finding appropriate scientists, engineers and specialists (even from abroad) to achieve this purpose becomes one of the most essential factors of a commercial success.

Secondly, different levels of development and incomes, asynchronic character of economic cycles cause, on the one hand, an increased demand for scientists and specialists of some selected professions in some countries and, on the other hand, their excess in others. This acts as a strong motivation for migration. If the process takes a continuous and large-scale character, preconditions for origination of "brain drain" phenomenon are thus formed.

Thirdly, a group of most different reasons such as wars, crises, ethnic conflicts, natural disasters, etc., also engender so-called forced migration flows. The origination of a new direction of East-West intellectual migration during recent years is a result, to a great extent, of the breakup of the Warsaw Pact, COMECON and disintegration of the Soviet Union combined with the cease of the "cold war" and origination of a new kind of partnership relations between the former allies. The transition to a new socio-economic arrangement, especially in the countries that used a "shock therapy" as a tool of their economic reforms has drastically reduced the demand for research, both basic and applied, reduced the national production output.

A great number of scientists and specialists, including high-skill ones, were deprived of their jobs; the remaining ones are faced with lower incomes, worsened job situation, disillusions about a successful career. In view of a very tense, complicated and uncertain political and economic situation in the former USSR countries flows of so-called ethnic migration originated (Jews, Germans, Greeks, Armenians, Meskheti Turks and others).

Fourthly, most clearly pronounced becomes such factor as the urge of an intellectual for self-realization the opportunities for which become now substantially wider in view of the progress in the area of human rights and transition from confrontation to partnership in international relations.

All these different motives for migration can be broadly classified into three large groups (blocks) the effect of which defines the scale and configuration of migration flows of "intellectual labour".

Economic block:
- a higher living standard and a higher salary in another (host) country;
- smaller expenditures and availability of subsidies for education in the country of origin;
- improper planning in education resulting in a long-time gap between the demand and the supply in favour of the latter in respect of scientists and specialists;
- a high level of unemployment in home country;
- economic disorder and a threat of a further decline of living standards.

Socio-Professional Block:
- difficulties in getting job according to one's profession;
- limited opportunities for a professional career for the specialist himself, lack of perspective for his children in home country;
- difficulties associated with retraining during structural changes, conversion of defense conversion, etc.;
- an insufficient prestige of some intellectual, especially technical, professions;
- public prejudices and social instability.

Some experts also mention additional factors of a professional character exerting certain influence on the rise of emigration moods. For example, Dr. A.Allakhverdyan, Institute of History of Natural and Technical Sciences, Russian Academy of Sciences, points to such motives, as:
- possibility of using modern scientific equipment for research and experimental work;
- possibility of using modern computer facilities;
- access to local and foreign professional literature;
- possibility of operative publication of the results of one's studies;
- possibility of public assessment and recognition of the results of one's scientific activity;
- possibility of practical implementation of one's scientific results;
- possibilities of establishing stable scientific relations and personal contacts with foreign colleagues.

Political-and-Ethnic Block:
- non-acceptance of the socio-political system and disbelief in the possibility of democratic transformations in home country;
- aggravation of inter-ethnic confrontation and conflicts;
- the urge for coming back to the historical homeland; reunification of families; mixed marriages.

In some cases only one of the above-mentioned factors in any of the blocks is enough to make the decision to emigrate to another country. When several motives from different blocks interrelate, migration booms appear which can bring about big international problems spread over large living spaces and causing destabilization of the equilibrium achieved in different regions.

Of course, the attitude to such a complicated and multifaceted problem could not be the same: positions and interests of global, national, regional structures and individual people could not coincide and, actually, in many cases were quite different.

Since the 60's two directions became clearly formulated in the literature in interpretation of "brain drain" phenomenon: internationalistic and nationalistic. [8].

In the opinion of those representing the first viewpoint, "brain drain" should be regarded first of all as a movement of "human capital" in the world market which is equally essential for economic progress as movement of other production factors. Likewise with capital, a human being wants to "invest" himself where he would be guaranteed that he'd get a maximum efficiency, security and minimum risk. [9]. For this reason, the proponents of the internationalistic approach considered that a state bearing expenses for education and professional training of its national specialists contributed not only to the national economy, but (through a system of migration of high-skill labour force) to the international progress as well, having at the same time the opportunity of availing itself of its fruit as a result of the inflow of foreign specialists.

The internationalistic concept "each for everybody" is opposed to the nationalistic concept "each for himself". Its adepts considered efforts and initiative taken by each individual state as a motive force of its scientific-and-technological and economic progress. That is why in the context of this concept "brain drain" is regarded as a factor of weakening of the state and of worsening prospects of its economic development.

It seems that the present-day realities are of such character that both standpoints have the right to exist, thus reflecting the pluralistic nature of societal processes, interests of different groups of states and strata of the population.

The "internationalists" hold that both sides, provided that they show their liability for compromises and for coordination of policies, can benefit from the progress of migration processes, especially from the perspective of long-term, rather than short-term, interests. They accuse the politicians who adhere to the "nationalistic" concept in lack of far-sightedness, in loss of the feeling of perspective. Of course, one can try to understand the fears of the leaders of countries willing to overcome backwardness and become equal partners in the global economy, to lose a great number of valuable personnel necessary in the most crucial stage of national rebirth. But in the long-run aspect, on condition of a purposeful policy, emigration processes can bring considerable benefits to home country.

High-skill specialists enriched with the foreign experience after coming back home can put a great contribution to the economy, science and culture of their homeland. Furthermore, the ethnic Diaspora formed during emigration can become later a kind of stronghold for their country facilitating access of their fellow countrymen to foreign markets including the host country's market. In their time, the immigrants from Italy, Japan, Gaiyana helped their countrymen to enter the American market and held their positions in it in this very manner.

The "nationalists" adhering to Roles's maximalist concept regard "brain drain" and its consequences primarily from the perspective of its influence on living standards of the population, especially of the most poor groups. According to Roles, mass emigration of labour force exerts an unquestionable detrimental effect on the remaining part of the population. In some cases the attention is paid to the fact that a mass immigration contributes to a growing unemployment and lowering wages of the local manpower. [10]. This is also added by the fact that in some cases immigrating specialists cannot get a job in the host country according to their profession and are bound to be satisfied with occasional earnings necessitating no skilled labour. This problem frequently faces foreigners from developing states and, quite recently, former citizens of post-socialist countries as well.

Such position to some extent is justified in respect of least developed and poor countries having socio-economic conditions sharply different from those of developed states. But is becomes less convincing relative to countries having levels of their development not so different. Moreover, the experience of a number of recently poor countries makes this allegation rather questionable. These countries encouraged trips of their citizens abroad for getting education, retraining, acquisition of up-to-date knowledge in hope for return of at least a portion of the emigrants. Substantially all newly industrialized countries (NIC) followed this policy. At the present time NIC elaborate a system of preferences making return of their specialists home attractive - providing better jobs, higher wages, good dwelling facilities). A certain role is given to a higher prestige of scientific, design and creative labour. For example, more than 2,000 scholars and engineers came back to the Republic of Korea by the middle of 1988. [11]. In the leading South-Korean conglomerates dozens of former emigrants with doctor's diploma of American universities worked in the mid-80's. The achievements of China in the nuclear sphere have become possible to a great extent to Chinese scholars who came back home after education and work in foreign, American in the first place, universities and companies.

A new turn of scientific and technological development, a growing interdependence of all states and aggravation of global problems strengthen the positions of "internationalists" in this dispute. The approach to a human being, his role in the labour process is also being changed. In this context the problem of "brain drain" becomes an integral part of the entire problem of the "human factor", thus increasing the role of the latter in investments associated with improvement of quality of labour force, amelioration of production process operations.

A comprehensive account of the "human input" made by leading US corporations already in 1960 showed that the organic composition of capital of "General Motors" was 2:1, that of "General Electric" was 1:1 and for "United States Steel" - the world leader of the most capital-intensive metallurgical industry - it was 2.6:1. [12].

Analysis of all costs of the formation of high-skill R&D labour force in the USA - direct expenses of a family for up-bringing young people, related labour of teachers and parents (during their non-working time), professional education and training, expenses of companies for retraining, etc. resulted in a conclusion that during the 80's average costs of preparation of one worker already exceeded $400,000 and that of a specialist - even $800,000. [13]. This points to a great role of labour of people in families, schools, universities educating a new generation of specialists for the post-industrial society imposing high requirements on the production culture and efficiency.

From this standpoint, emigration means, of course, direct losses for home country. Indirect losses are also essential, since an outflow of a great number of specialists decelerates production growth, narrows opportunities of export of goods with a high level of the scientific component. The departure of noticeable numbers of the most professionally skilled part of the society can lower the general level of the production and social culture in the country, affect its intellectual and civilization potential.

At the same time, an opposite trend is observed: acquisition of foreign experience and expertise through mass inflows of foreign specialists and return of emigrants to their homeland, their money transfers and taxes on higher incomes can reduce national expenditures for the solution of vitally important domestic problems and accelerate this process.

The above-discussed problems are far from fully describing all the aspects of the process of mobility of scientists and specialists at the present time, but their complexity and scale, contradicting character of interests of the participants involved make necessary elaborating a proper methodological approach to assessment of a combined effect of "brain drain" on different levels: international (global), national (state), commercial (from the perspective of an industry, a company) and individual. The most urgent and complicated for the system of international relations now is the interstate level, i.e. an assessment, though approximate, of the gains and losses of the states involved in the present-day migration flows.

1.3. METHODOLOGY OF ASSESSMENT OF THE EFFECT OF INTELLECTUAL MIGRATION ON COUNTRIES INVOLVED

There is no unified approach in the literature to assessment of "brain-drain" phenomenon. When it took a large-scale character, a negative approach prevailed. The appropriate estimates were made exclusively from the standpoint of economic efficiency (cost of education of emigrants in the home country, weakening of the national scientific-and-technological potential, benefits lost due to departure of specialists needed for the country, etc.).

In contrast to the "pessimistic" approach another point of view was formed according to which migration of scientists and specialists can be useful not only for the recipient country. Proponents of this standpoint argued that emigration contributes to resolving the problem of unemployment among the remaining scientists and specialists, while emigrants substantially improve their well-being. In addition, the acquaintance with foreign experience can be very useful for the country if a part of emigrants come back to their home country for permanent residence or even for vacations. To prove this, an example of Chinese nuclear scientists who came back to China after their work in the United States is frequently given.

Unfortunately, advocates of both "pessimistic" and "optimistic" approaches cannot quantitatively substantiate the advantages of their position. The attempts to calculate all the gains or losses cannot be regarded successful, since they necessitate numerous assumptions and estimation indicators which, in many cases, enable both sides to insist on their reasonable approach based on the results obtained. Political, social, cultural factors, as well as individual preferences, the changing situation within the country and outside should be taken into consideration in addition to economic factors. Due to the above-mentioned reasons any quantitative calculations of losses and/or gains from migration flows can be regarded only as approximate estimates enabling determination of the trends prevailing in this very complicated social phenomenon.

Methodologically, emigration is categorized into temporary and permanent ones. In the former case it is sometimes called a "positive mobility". It is assumed that a temporary departure of a scholar or specialist abroad for a period of two-three years now becomes a very important component of the system of improving their qualifications and, hence, brings certain gains to their home countries , facilitating their integration into the global scientific-and-technological community. Such geographic mobility is interrelated with sectoral one: through foreign trips and missions the country not only disseminates new knowledge and known R&D results, but also gains an access to scientific and technological achievements which it needs.

Nearly all kinds of short-term contacts of scholars going abroad are useful for their country: scientific conferences, seminars, symposia, colloquia, etc., as well as joint research in foreign laboratories and research centers. Practice shows that temporary migration of R&D specialists also enables their country to acquire foreign experience, especially in erection and assembling heavy-duty industrial installations, during their work in transnational corporations.

A different approach is necessary in assessing effects of a permanent emigration. A mass-scale departure of scientific personnel (and in some branches of science - even of a small number of prominent scholars) is a loss for their country. First of all, its scientific and technological potential is weakened which, in addition to deceleration of economic growth and hindering education of young scientists and specialists, results in additional obstacles in following the course for integration into the world scientific and technological community. Secondly, the expenses borne by the state for up-bringing, education and training of emigrants remain non-reimbursed. Thirdly, the country is also faced with opportunity costs equal to the expected contribution of the emigrants to the economy and science of the country on condition of their refusal from going abroad. Fourthly, the possibility on-hindered emigration of a non-hindered emigration can complicate staffing local educational and research institutions, engineering boards and enterprises with qualified scientific and technological personnel.

The above-given scheme provides only a partial description of the process. It is obvious that along with the actual and exacted losses associated with a long-term emigration other factors should also be taken into consideration. If a crisis situation takes place in the country in the human component of the R&D potential (the state cannot support the over-grown and finding no full utilization state sector of science; educational institutions cannot hire highly qualified professors and scientists due to an insufficient funding; industry and sphere of servicing do not demand them due to the drop of production and reduction of consumption), certain corrections should be made in the calculations based on the above considerations. It is possible that a part of emigrants who left the country in such situation have done this not for material considerations, but for the sake of maintaining their qualification and possibility of self-realization. They can come home after coming of their country out of the crisis and appearance of urgent demand for their knowledge and experience. For this reason, their return should be regarded already as "import" of knowledge (with the account of gains from their activity) and, accordingly, be deducted from the calculated losses.

Emigrants frequently keep contacts with their relatives and other persons remaining in their home country, support them financially (send money, parcels, etc.). Various charges, fees, etc. which should be paid by the specialists leaving the country should be also taken into consideration.

In respect of the territory of the former Soviet Union the specific situation should be taken into consideration, namely: along with the migration outflow from Russia there originates a "substituent" inflow of the Russian-speaking population from "near abroad". Until relations between the CIS countries are brought into a civilized frame and the conflicts in the near abroad are ceased, the effect of this counter-current wave of migration of scientists and specialists to Russia should be taken into account. In many cases they can replace the specialists leaving Russia. In view of an excess of high-qualification R&D personnel formed in the country at the present moment, it is quite reasonable to consider such substitution as a partial compensation of losses, because it would be hardly possible to find jobs for immigrants from the near abroad according to their professions without "freeing" vacancies by specialists emigrating abroad.

Therefore, in view of the specific situation in Russia nowadays and in the short run the problem of migration in this country and in many developing states becomes a very complicated social phenomenon influenced by a number of trends that contradict to each other and, in turn, provide an ambiguous effect on the socio-economic situation in the country. Not all these processes are apt to a quantitative presentation and, in many cases where it is possible in principle, no regular statistical monitoring of such phenomena is carried out. For this reason, one has to limit himself to several large aggregated indicators subsequently added by expert assessments.

We suggest that in its general form the damage caused for a given country by a mass exodus of scientists and specialists be expressed in the following manner:

$$D = (Eupbr.+ed. + OCex. + RL) - (IR + RR + P),$$

wherein:

- Eupbr.+ ed. - expenses for upbringing, education and training of a scholar or a specialist multiplied by the number of emigrated persons;
- OCex. - opportunity costs, i.e. gains lost due to exclusion of the emigrated scholars and specialists from the economic activity in their home country;

- RL - related losses: lowering of the R&D potential, worsened quality of products and lower qualification level of the personnel due to a shortage, especially in the province, of skilled specialists and scientists;
- IR - incomes obtained as a result of return of a portion of the emigrants to their country. It is calculated like Eupbr.+ ed.
- RR - revenues as a result of reinvolvement of the former emigrants in the national economy less the period of time passed outside the home country;
- P - payments to the state budget as various charges and fees by emigrants, as well as their money transfers, capital contributions to joint enterprises, etc.

The obtained results need a further interpretation. For example, the division of emigration into ethnic and labour one: in the former case the probability of re-emigration is much lower, while total losses, all other things being equal, are greater. Social factors should be also taken into account, in particular level of unemployment and incomes of different groups of emigrants, conditions of interstate relations with the countries of immigration. These approximated calculations would better reflect the actual pattern of emigration with continuous improvement of the data monitoring.

Many international organizations such as ILO, UNESCO and UNCTAD are engaged in a quantitative analysis of "brain drain" wastes and gains. In 1975 the UNCTAD Secretariat assessed, through a series of complicated calculations, the economic effect of "brain drain" from developing states to industrially developed countries for both sides. [1]

The quantitative analysis was based on the data on the growth and losses of incomes from the inflow of high-qualification cadres to developed countries and their outflow from developing ones. The calculations were effected using the following four parameters:

- Opportunity costs (OC) - for developing countries these are wastes of high-skill cadres due to "brain drain";
- Gains obtained (GO) - for developed states - additional revenues due to the inflow of high-skill personnel from developing countries;

- Domestic expenditures (DE) - expenses borne by developing countries for education and training of the personnel emigrated to developed states;
- Alternative expenditures - would be costs of training of their own personnel by developed countries in case of absence of the inflow of labour force from developing states.

To assess the general effect of "brain drain" process for each group of countries, it is necessary to take into account various possible combinations of these four parameters. One can suggest two methods for calculation of the effect of "brain drain": from the "gain" and "waste" standpoints. Usually, in calculations of a short-term effect the GO are compared with the OC (i.e. losses of developing countries with gains of developed ones), since within short time periods it is difficult to determine the parameters characterizing costs of training cadres (or savings on them). Within longer periods comparable with time limits for training specialists the parameters DE and AE are taken into consideration. It should be noted that the use of these formulae is possible with quite a lot of various assumptions and with the account of the partners' specificity.

Calculations made according to the above-described method (averaged data) have shown that, for example, the net income of the United States owing to inflow of high-skill specialists from developing countries in 1970 was equal to $3.7 bln. [2]

The total losses of the countries exporting their specialists can be even higher, since there are estimates according to which the "output" from a high-skill scientist or engineer is by 20 times greater than the "input" in him, i.e. expenses for his training. But if such engineers and scientists come back home, they thus reduce the income of the host country and make contribution to the progress of their own homeland.

Furthermore, quantitative assessments do not take into account social, political, ethnic factors which quite frequently might become the most decisive for an emigrant. That is why quantitative parameters of "gains-losses" have rather empirical nature and are incapable of giving a comprehensive assessment of such a complicated and multifaceted phenomenon as "brain drain".

The "brain drain" problem is closely related to the system of taxation in the emigrants' country of origin. The necessity for taxation of emigrants is explained, on the one hand, by the fact that the specialists who left the country had relatively high salaries in their homeland and, accordingly, paid high taxes. Their departure, therefore, results in lowered payments to the state budget.

On the other hand, migrants, especially from poor countries, have relatively high incomes in the country of their residence which, in their economic nature, are equivalent to a rent. For this reason, there is an opinion that such "economic" rent should be subjected to taxation in the interests of social justice. However, if this tax is too high, it would force the specialists living abroad to change their citizenship. At a moderate tax rate a mutually beneficial compromise is reached: a specialist is interested in continuing his work abroad and his home country has also certain gains, since it gets currency revenues and still retains its specialist's citizenship. Hence, each country has to define the tax rate itself, depending on particular circumstances. Philippines can be mentioned as an example where in the mid-70's a tax of 1 to 3 percent of the total income was charged from all those working abroad, irrespective of their profession and qualification. [3]

C.R. McConnel and S.L. Brue in their book "Economics" took an attempt to assess the effect of migration on several economic levels. [4]

The authors analyze the consequences of emigration from Mexico to the United States for both countries. On the global level (from the standpoint of world economy) the inflow of Mexican labour force (skilled personnel especially) ensures an increment of the US national product in a value greater than its loss in Mexico due to the departure of emigrants. This enables the authors to state that the real volume of national product in the whole world is increasing. However, in the interstate interaction the donor country has losses, while the acceptor country gets advantages. From a company's standpoint the pattern is the following: business in the US gains from immigration due to acquisition of inexpensive labour force, while emigration brings damage to Mexico's national economy. A mass-scale emigration gives rise to a trend of reduction of an average wage level in the USA and, on the contrary, its increase in Mexico.

This, though simplified, model gives a general understanding of a "multi-layered" character of migration processes. For an individual immigrant it is important that despite the lowering of an average wage level in the USA, it is still higher than that in Mexico. The effect of taxation, money transfers and a number of other factors should be also taken into consideration. Besides, if a chronic unemployment still exists in Mexico, emigration cannot be regarded as losses. Therefore, any study of migration of scholars and specialists should be based on the entire complex of political, economic, social, ethnic, cultural and other relevant factors.

The conclusions resulting from the above considerations are, in our opinion, merely first steps along the way of resolving the problem under discussion. Up to now, it was possible only to trace the dominating trends, to call for pooling efforts of all countries concerned, as well as for cooperation within the framework of international organizations for a comprehensive evaluation of the "brain drain" phenomenon which has become an integral component of the contemporary international relations.

1.4. SOCIO-ECONOMIC IMPLICATIONS OF INTELLECTUAL EMIGRATION

Emigration of high-qualification personnel from Russia via different departure channels is going on and, despite its various assessments and different approaches, brings certain losses to the country. When a considerable part of specialists leave the homeland temporarily or forever for various reasons, migration takes a specific dimension and starts to affect numerous aspects of the social life of the donor country. If this phenomenon acquires a mass scale and gains momentum, it might bring about substantial material and socio-economic problems resulting in irreversible negative processes in the society.

The departure of a great number of scientists or even of several individual scholars can affect the state of national science and R&D policy. The nation's R&D potential becomes substantially weakened, especially in view of long-term repercussions related to training of new generations of scientists and specialists. In general, the country can deprive itself of a stratum of people indispensable for keeping up the process of national scientific and economic reproduction, preserving the required social structure and balance within the framework of the selected course of socio-economic progress.

Despite the conditional character of the quantitative evaluation of material damage, the donor country loses investments already effected into education and training of cadres, as well as potential revenues from the non-realized highly-qualified labour. Estimates of Russia's losses from emigration vary from $60 to 75 bln. a year. By the beginning of 1991 the damage to the former USSR from emigration of highly educated elite was as high as nearly $100 bln. According to the latest estimates by the Commission for Education of Council of Europe, the "brain drain" losses of Russia will amount to $50. [1]. Calculations made according to UN procedure (deduction of the total of direct and indirect expenditures for training of emigrating specialists from the gross national product plus potentially lost revenues resulting from economic activity of emigrants in their homeland if they stayed there) by the beginning of 1991 show that the country loses $300,000 due to the departure of one R&D specialist.

A simple arithmetic calculation of the forecast data (see Chapter II) can illustrate Russia's losses from "brain drain" for one year or a longer period. These figures are counted in billions (US dollars).

Of course, this is a complicated and multi-faceted phenomena which also has its "silver lining". One of the positive aspects - return of specialists who got new knowledge and skills, international contacts and access to international foreign information, as well as experience of scientific and business activity in a market environment. Besides, national diaspora originated in emigration can and do become a kind of support for donor countries. They assist their fellow countrymen in getting access to foreign markets, they can also bring merely financial benefits to their former homeland through transfers of money to their relatives living there. Especially this is the case of labour migration. Revenues of certain countries - exporters of manpower - from this kind of remittance amount to several billion dollars. For example, in 1992 Egypt received $6,104 mln. from its nationals working abroad, Brazil - $2,047 mln.; Mexico - $2,270 mln.; Portugal - $4,794 mln; Pakistan - $2,772 mln.;, Columbia - $1,741 mln.; Australia - $1,535 mln. [2].

However, positive post-effects of emigration occur with a time lag of 10 to 15 years. At the present moment Russia does not have a fully developed mechanism of taxation of people working on contracts and of hiring specialists for work abroad, as well as of an efficient system of their money transmittances to homeland - it has only insignificant benefits from labour migration. Today Russia has tangible losses from emigration of scientists and specialists and this situation is likely to prevail in the foreseeable future.

But especially appreciable damage resulting from a mass exodus of specialists is brought to the intellectual level of the society, qualitative composition of its labour resources both at the present time, and in the average- and long-term perspective. Scientific and technical intelligentsia leaves the country which thus loses most creative part of its intellectual elite - physicists, mathematicians, biologists, programmers, as well as engineers and technicians. According to estimates by Academician A.Andreev, Deputy Director of Kapitsa Institute of physical problems and Vice-President of Russian Academy of Sciences, about 40% of top-level physicists-theoreticians and over 12% of physicists-experimentalists left the former USSR temporarily or forever. [3]. Losses caused by exodus of such people from their homeland in many cases are difficult to measure both qualitatively and quantitatively.

For example, A.Zinberg, former shift engineer at Moscow factory for repair of home radioelectronic appliances, now US citizen, is an author of more than 30 major inventions out of 100 made throughout the world in the field of high-resolution TV - television of the 21-st century. With his departure, also for the reason that his inventions were non-recognized and unclaimed in his home country, Russia lost the opportunity of an equal-right participation in the international "club" of inventors and manufacturers of such high-tech products and with time it will be bound to spend huge money for importation of appropriate technologies and equipment, as well as final articles from abroad (including the USA), because of its lagging-behind in this area due to the loss of an active "generator" of new, promising and efficient technical ideas.

Or, former Russian biologist E.Shpaer, now living in the USA and working at Stanford University, using his Soviet-period expertise in application of computer technology to molecular biology, made a great progress in AIDS diagnosis. "Specific character of his education and interests gave a new dimension to our research" - said Dr. J.Malins, Head of the Department of Microbiology and Immunology of Stanford University. Hence, in this case Russia lost its chance to occupy leading positions in such important area of medical research.

Unfortunately, the list of such examples is too long for Russia.

Especially heavy consequences Russia faces in connection with emigration of talents from the area of military and dual-use technologies, both rankers and leaders of disintegrating scientific schools and research centers in such fields as space technology and engineering, radioelectronics, information technologies, genetic engineering, etc. Only in the USA over a dozen of full and corresponding members of the former USSR Academy of Sciences (in their number is Academician R.Sagdeev, ex-Director of the Institute of

Space Research) found their jobs; in NASA more than 100 former Soviet space-technology specialists are employed, in Israel nearly 90% of specialists of its military-industrial complex are former Soviet citizens. [4]. It is quite obvious that such situation strengthens general economic, R&D and military might of foreign countries and weakens national economic potential of Russia, its military-industrial complex (MIC).

One of the reasons of this phenomenon is the ongoing conversion of this complex which, unfortunately, has no reasonable concept interrelated with the national military doctrine, strategic interests of Russia's national security in general. As a result, the recently powerful R&D potential of the MIC is in a critical situation, close to destruction. According to the RF Committee for Defense Industries, in 1992 nearly 200,000 scientists left Russia's defense complex; around 350 defence-oriented research centers and design offices are subject to conversion and re-orientation to civilian research. The aerospace component of Russia's MIC alone lost more than 1/3 of its doctors and candidates of sciences in 1992 and the first half of 1993. During 1992-1993 30% of scientists and specialists left the MIC of Russia. [5]. Some of them emigrated to the "far abroad".

One of the most refined forms of "brain drain" in the case of the former Soviet Union is employment of local personnel by foreign companies resident in its territory, by way of establishment of joint ventures, leasing or buying entire research and development centers, industrial enterprises, etc. (which is now allowed by the ongoing privatization reform), i.e. without going of such personnel abroad. A paradoxical situation is observed: while remaining at home, a considerable part of national R&D specialists are excluded from the domestic economy and become being partly or fully engaged in activities in the interests of foreign countries, foreign science, production and market as if they were staying there. This relates to both basic and applied research, development and production.

For example, a well-known US company "Procter and Gamble" has, in fact, rented the entire Institute of Biomedical Chemistry, Russian Academy of Medical Sciences, for 5 years with the purpose of employing Russian scientists in studies of protease enzymes, computer formulation of medicinal preparations, synthesis of antiallergenic agents. Despite the fact that intellectual property rights belong to both sides, it is quite clear, that in view of lack of investments, pilot and production capacities in the Russian pharmaceutical industry all commercial benefits from such partnership, at an average monthly salary of the Russian personnel of $50 [6], would be on the American partner's side, to say nothing about a long-time (5 years) exclusion of one of the leading Russian pharmaceutical research centers from the solution of more urgent scientific problems (other than those contracted by "Procter and Gamble") associated with the development and production of medicines badly needed by the Russian population right now, taking into consideration the current critical situation in pharmaceuticals in this country.

This example shows that within the framework of this particular form of "brain drain" the interests of professional communities and individuals do not always agree with the state-national interests of the home country; minor this-minute benefits of individuals prevail in many cases over more important immediate and long-term interests of the nation and positive effects for small professional groups are incomparable with possible negative consequences for the entire population.

This sophisticated form of "brain drain" is very suitable for foreign counterparts, since in addition to substantial savings resulting from the use of local production facilities, research equipment, instrumentation and materials they save much money on wages and salaries of specialists, development of social infrastructure for them in case they were immigrants and have other advantages such as lack of social tension in the professional community of a foreign country in case of inflow of ex-Soviet immigrants, etc. On the other hand, from the Russian economy the best specialists are withdrawn (in many cases foreign partners employ local personnel through competition and special test systems) for work in foreign companies and joint ventures. They are relatively highly paid comparing to general salary level in local research and production organizations (but much less than in a foreign country at the same level of professional qualification and skills). This engenders certain social discontent due to the difference in earnings of those employed in foreign-owned and local organizations, or even at the same institution with a part of its employees being paid from local financial sources and others - from appropriate funds of a foreign partner.

Describing cooperation of a well-known American company "Bell Laboratories" with the Institute of General Physics, Russian Academy of Sciences, the "New York Times" wrote, in particular: "Like in other research institutes getting American assistance, at the Institute of General Physics where over 1,200 researchers are employed, they do not want to pay a salary equivalent to $132 a year to one researcher and $70,000 to another having a subsidy from the USA. This gap can cause envy in Russian laboratories, and when the term of contract with the American company expires, a suddenly-rich scientist again becomes poor." [7].

To avoid negative consequences of "brain drain", it is necessary to exert a positive influence on its reasons and motive factors. Unfortunately, it is not always practiced in Russia and other countries of the former Soviet Union. Indeed, why could Western companies offer a prestigious work at their leading research and production centers abroad to winners of the 3-rd computer Olympiad in Moscow (citizens of the CIS), whereas in our countries no appropriate jobs and work and homelife conditions were found? [8]. Meanwhile, they are the "golden fund", elite of domestic programmers-actual promoters of scientific and technological progress. This is only one minor example of a thoughtless wasting of our own intellectual resources, criminal pushing up of "brain drain" abroad. It is a subject for reflection for managers of agencies responsible for the progress of science and technology in the CIS, especially in Russia.

It is not incidentally that in view of the above-mentioned and other negative consequences of "brain drain" many Russian experts and analysts consider it as a factor of threat to technological security of Russia, its national security in general.

Historically, it turned out so that Russia, along with the US, Germany and France, is a stable leader in basic research during the recent hundred years. A unique "microcosmos" was formed in Russia enabling to guess that at minimum initial measures of support the subsequent civilized export of basic scientific ideas would enable not only preservation of science itself, but to contribute considerably to the progress of the national economy in general. One of the components of this "microcosmos" represents scientific personnel engaged in basic research whose loss might result in its destruction and/or its use for the progress of science and economy of foreign countries.

However, the most apt to emigration are representatives of basic science. Among scientific areas especially affected by emigration, mathematics and computer science can be mentioned. The international character of the mathematical language and a high demand for Russian programmers makes the "brain drain" problem for this category of scientists ranking first in the total outflow of intellectuals. Their number is as high as 15-20% of the total number of emigrants. [9].

Another group of scientists heading the list of would-be emigrants includes representatives of some leading areas of biology and medicine.

Of course, frightening forecasts about hundreds thousands of Russian scientists leaving the country are not justified by reality, but a sober assessment of the scale and professional structure of the intellectual emigrants cannot but cause a deep concern. The country is left by the most actively working youth and average-age scholars who already achieved high scientific results and are well-known both in the country and abroad for their publications. The major part of scientists of Russian Academy of Sciences emigrated from Russia abroad for a permanent residence have a scientific degree of Candidate (55.9%) and Doctor (16.2%) of Science. Nearly half (48.5) of the emigrants is under 40-years age. [10].

Another evidence proving the steadiness of the trend of amassing emigration of intellectuals in the coming short-run period is the assessment of emigration moods of students of a number of Moscow institutes effected in 1992. The poll covered 2,200 students of "elite" professions of Moscow State University, Moscow Aviation Institute, Moscow Institute of Physical Engineering, Moscow Institute of Electronic Engineering. Nearly 56% of the questioned students answered that they were going to leave the country, 7% told that they were ready to do so as soon as possible. The poll enables a conclusion that representatives of social sciences are less liable to emigration. As regards motivation of emigration, the poll revealed the following results [11]:

- 14% of students of humanities and 18% of would-be engineers are attracted by life and work abroad;
- 60% of students of humanities and 42% of engineering institutes would like to see the world, to get acquainted with the way of life abroad and come back home;
- 24% of students of humanities and 31% of would-be engineers want to work for some time in a foreign country, to earn some money and come back to their homeland;
- 31% of students of humanitarian institutes and 17% of students of engineering institutes want to obtain education abroad;

- 9% of humanities students and 16% of would-be engineers would like to start their private business abroad.

Representatives of humanitarian professions prefer emigration to Western Europe, while technical specialists want to go to the USA.

Scholars and specialists go abroad for a temporary (short- or long-term) work on their own initiative. According to forecasts for 1993, 4% of scientists and researchers wanted to do so. [12]. It can be expected that some of them would prefer to stay abroad, since their knowledge and qualification presumably find no use at home. But this very type of migration is more adaptable to organizational, legal and socio-economic regulation on both national and international levels and this category of migrants deserves a greater attention.

It cannot be allowed that losses of intellectuals due to emigration would exceed a certain "critical mass" limit beyond which the system of reproduction of scientific and technical cadres gets broken and quality of the national R&D potential is impaired. In the "Fundamentals of the Concept of Scientific and Technological Policy of the Russian Federation" elaborated by the RF Ministry of Science and Technological Policy it is said that for an irreversible degradation of the Russian science it is sufficient that 10-15% of the most promising and talented scientists of young and average age leave the country.

The loss of such a great number of high-skill specialists is especially sensitive during crisis periods when a one-sided orientation a mere entrepreneurial skill is not enough for a success - an inflow of specialists with analytical thinking and experience in R&D activities is necessary for the industry and sphere of services.

Emigration of scientists and specialists can result in disintegration of research teams and schools including those having advanced knowledge in the most progressive areas of R&D; it noticeably hinders implementation of the results of priority studies, lowers efficiency of investments into basic and applied sciences. The base for training high-qualification specialists indispensable for retaining the society's intellectual potential is undermined and the labour market of scientific and technical personnel is disorganized.

A mass-scale emigration is not always advantageous for the entire world scientific community. Some scientists and specialists cannot find job according to their profession and qualification, they are forced to change the sphere of their professional activity so as to earn their living in any permissible way. In this case "brain drain" turns into "brain waste". Russia loses her scientists and this loss is not compensated by gains obtained by the world science or by the receiving countries' economies.

However, according to some experts, still greater damage to the socio-economic progress of the country is brought by a so-called internal "brain drain" or an outflow of specialists from scientific, design and other organizations to administrative and production structures, i.e. shift to a less complicated professional activity. At the present time up to 30% of managers of new commercial structures are former scientists and high-skill technical specialists. [13].

In total, during 1986-1992 the number of employed in the R&D sphere reduced by 1.1 mln. persons, i.e. over this period the drop of employment in science was about 22%. If these data are regarded from the sectoral point of view, the number of employed in academic science (within the system of Russian Academy of Sciences - RAS) reduced over these years by 24.4%, industrial science - by 30.4%, university science - by 11%. [14]. Since 1992 the process of internal "brain drain" acquired an accelerated character. By the beginning of 1993 the number of persons employed in science and its servicing was 2.1 mln. vs. 2.8 mln. on January 1, 1992. [15]. Such reduction rates are close to critical ones and can result in a negative or hyper-mobility.

The exodus from science occurs against the background of a substantial discontinuation of inflow of youth in the R&D sphere. For example, according to the data of observation of a number of scientific and technological organizations in Moscow in 1992 they hired only 32 young specialists which constituted less than 1% of the total number of persons employed in R&D work of these organizations. This trend is most illustrative in the RAS system. The recruitment of post-graduates there in 1989 was 3,500 persons, in 1991 - 2,000; in 1992 - slightly over 1,000 persons; in 1993 for all areas of R&D in RAS less than 800 post-graduates were recruited. [16].

The sphere of education and training also suffers heavily from a considerable internal "brain drain". The number of professors and lecturers who left their pedagogical activities is about 20-30% The loss of scholars from educational institutions who usually combine their research activity with teaching, lowers the level and quality of education, and to some extent defines the scale of subsequent admission of students for education. Due to a specific character of the sphere of education, negative effects of this process will reveal themselves only after 10-15 years.

The "internal migration" from science is caused by a number of socio-economic factors such as considerable difference in labour payment in science compared to other spheres of the economy. In 1991 salaries in science were by 7% less than average ones in the national economy, in 1992 - by 30%, in 1993 - beginning of 1994 they were by more than 2 times lower. Among other factors one can also mention impossibility of realization of one's creative abilities under crisis conditions in science, reduction of the number of employed in a given branch of science and industry, growing unemployment among researchers and professors, etc. These reasons still prevail in Russia and the process of exodus of professionally-skilled personnel from science is still ongoing.

This double-nature outflow of cadres from the R&D sphere has multiple negative effects for the country. As a result of internal "brain drain" the heaviest losses are characteristic for engineering and technological sciences, economics, management, pedagogics; to a lesser extent it relates to law and some other humanities. The external outflow includes specialists of other disciplines: mathematics, chemistry, biology, physics, informatics, medicine. The combination of both currents results in escape of persons who define social, economic and political health of the society, the level of development of national scientific and production potentials, state of learning and education, quality and scale of medical care.

The internal migration which, as to its scale, is now greater than emigration, aggravates the damage from the external "drain", since it results in a loss of a potential professional value of a specialist, the more so that those who leave science and technology possess qualities indispensable under new conditions, namely: entrepreneurship, managerial abilities, industriousness, etc. Of course, their labour in other spheres will be also productive for the economy, but their potential for the country's R&D will not be fully realized. Such waste of intellectual potential results in a lowered level and quality of R&D, reduction of their scale, diminution of prestige of research labour. The possibilities are reduced for studies in critical areas solving most urgent problems of the national economy. It can eventually result in deceleration of innovation growth rates, loss of priorities in the most important R&D areas, growing gap between the national and world science.

Spreading of emigration moods, as well as the desire of a certain part of the population to leave the country at the first opportunity also produce a detrimental effect on the socio-psychological state of the society. The emigration-oriented thinking of scientists (especially their middle-level category), state and economic bodies, business men becomes a motive force which is so strong that the majority of emigrants go abroad with the desire to stay there for a permanent residence without thinking about their future social status and being agree to obtain any job. The people willing to emigrate forever or to leave on a temporary contract reflect the reaction of the formerly closed society to the newly acquired freedom, compensation for long years of strict limitations and severe state control of going out of the country.

A poll among Moscow scientists (May-June, 1991) showed that 6% out of them declared their desire to go abroad for a permanent residence. In the group of up to 30 years such persons numbered 21%, in the group of 30-50 years - about 5%. [17.]

The emigration moods get stronger when there is an opportunity of going abroad on a temporary contract for a predetermined period of time. Such readiness was expressed by 51% of the questioned researchers which together with those ready to leave forever is already a great figure of 57%. The emigration inclination, therefore, touches upon many specialists and defines the scale of potential migrants.

Prevailing of such moods, especially among youth, the desire to realize one's dreams results in a changing social position of a certain part of the population. The life-stimulating motives disappear along with hopes and faith in the future of the home country, motivation for labour gets weakened, likewise the interest for creative activity and self-improvement. Moreover, due to a general dissatisfaction with the life at home and impossibility of leaving homeland (for different reasons) there occurs either lowering of personal claims or a change of life priorities and interests in general, a growing depression is also probable. An acute dissatisfaction with life at home is felt due to lack of demand for personal knowledge, threat of "intellectual unemployment", necessity of changing the activity area.

The problem of emigration, despite all the attention it deserves and the extensive debates around it nowadays, is still expecting a proper assessment. This subject needs profound and extensive studies adapted to specific conditions of Russia and former republics of ex-USSR, since processes of emigration from Russia occur against the background of so many inter-related internal and external factors that all general regularities known so far got substantially changed and have to be reconsidered to become applicable to Russia.

At the present time, under conditions of political instability, economic crisis, inter-ethnic and territorial conflicts in Russia, the socio-economic effects of "brain drain" are not perceived as they should be. The apprehension of emigration problems is shaped under the influence of some ideal considerations incompatible with the real consequences, especially in the long-run perspective.

Meanwhile, emigration of R&D personnel from Russia is not ceasing and apparently will continue during the current decade. It is likely that its character would change - the flow of persons going abroad for a permanent residence is decreasing, while labour emigration is growing. The main reasons boosting this process are of economic nature.

Consequently, the economy which should be developed by a rational use of the scientific-and-technological cadres is responsible itself for engendering the main factors pushing up emigration. The paradox of the situation resides in that Russia provides nowadays more promising opportunities for aggressive, industrious and talented people than any other country in the world.

These multi-faceted emigration processes in Russia require a purposeful state policy for regulation of migration flows on a sound legal base both inside the country and in relations with the states of destination for emigrants. This could provide certain guarantees for Russian nationals abroad, ensure the required social protection and thus create appropriate preconditions for their coming home in future.

REFERENCES

Section 1.1 & 1.2

1. " Economist", July 26, 1969, p.14.
2. Cf. UNCTAD, TD/B/AC.II/25/Rev. 1.
3. Immigrant Scientists and Engineers in United States. A Study of Characteristics and Attitudes., NSF, 1973, p.16.
4. The Reverse Transfer of Technology: A Survey of Its Main Features, Causes and Policy Implications., UN, N.Y., 1977, p.5.
5. Ibid., p.5.
6. Science and Engineering Personnel. A National Overview., NSF, 198), p.48.
7. "World Development", 1975, No.10, pp.677-715.
8. W.Adams. The Brain Drain., New York, Macmillan, 1968.
9. H.Johnson. Economic Policy Towards Less Developed Countries. Washington, 1968; Third World Quaterly, Vol.1, No.3, July 1979.
10. Ibid.; International Conference "East-West Mobility of Scientists and Engineers", Vienna, February 18-19, 1993.
11. "Financial Times", May 25, 1988.
12. "World Economy and International Relations" ("Mirovaya Ekonomika i Mezhdunarodnye Otnosheniya"), 1991, No.11, pp. 8-24.
13. Ibid.

Section 1.3

1. The Reverse Transfer of Technology. UNCTAD, 1975, TD/B/11/25, Rev.1.
2. Op.cit., p.2.
3. G.F.M. Sicat. A Survey of Problems and Policies in the Philippines. UNCTAD, Geneva, TD/B/C6/AC 4/5, 1977, p.9.

4. C.R. McConnel, S.L. Brue. Economics. Principles, Problems and Policies. p.311, 316.

Section 1.4

1. "Rossijskiye Vesti", 16.02.1994, p.8.
2. International Financial Statistics. February 1994, IMF, Washington, 1994.
3. "Izvestiya", 03.02.1992.
4. "Segodnya" ("Today"), 17.02.1994, p.9; "Rossijskiye Vesti", 20.10.1993, p.11.
5. "Reforma", January 1994, No.1, p.12.
6. "Izvestiya", 09.02.1994.
7. "New-York Times. Weekly Review", Business, February 2-15, 1993, pp. B1-B2.
8. "Radical", No.24, July 3, 1992, p.10.
9. "Izvestiya", 15.02.1994.
10. "Brain Drain" in Modern Russia: Domestic and International Aspects. UNESCO-ROSTE, Moscow, 1992, p.218.
11. Program for migration studies. Institute for Employment Problems. Population migration laboratory, RAND Corp., USA. "Brain Drain": potential, problems, prospects. Issue II, Moscow, 1993, pp.100-144.
12. "Poisk", No.9, 1993, p.5.
13. "Poisk", No.9, 1993; "Izvestiya" No.81, 30.04.1994.
14. "Poisk", No.9, 1993, p.5.
15. "Poisk", No.14, 1994, p.1.
16. "Reforma", January 1994, No.1, p.13.
17. "Brain Drain" in Modern Russia... Op.cit., p.218.

CHAPTER II

"BRAIN DRAIN" FROM RUSSIA

2.1. RUSSIAN SCIENCE: PRESENT STATE AND CHALLENGES OF THE 90'S

The present state of Russian science is one of the most important objects of analysis in the study of the problem of intellectual emigration from this country. At the same time, crisis of science and the R&D sphere in general is not the only and, probably, not the main reason of this phenomenon, because this crisis in itself is merely a derivative of the profound socio-economic and political crisis that gripped substantially all sides of life of Russian society. Analysis of this truly global phenomenon is beyond the scope of this book. Nevertheless, it is expedient and logical to disclose some of its aspects emphasizing specific features of the environment in which Russian science has to exist. This is especially true in view of the fact that "brain drain" occurs not only from the R&D, but also from other spheres of Russia's national economy.

During several recent years Russia's economy is in a deep recession. Drop of production output, growth of inflation and unemployment, investment paralysis, crisis of non-payment, related rupture of production links and bartering of exchanges between enterprises and regions of this country - all these and many other negative have become usual, everyday phenomena of Russian economy. But what is most important - a swift decline of living standards and quality of life of the population is observed. This is revealed in a rapid reduction of real wages which, according to official data, over the period of 1990-1993 decreased by more than 2.6 times. [1].

During four years the proportion of least paid workers and employees increased from 5 to 37.8%, whereas that of moderately- and highly-paid people reduced from 47.4 to 18.3%. [2]. "These data - "Izvestiya", a newspaper liberal to the government of Russia, writes - clearly demonstrate a mass pauperization of working people due to washing-out of middle-class strata, their shift towards the less better-off and nearing the most poor groups of the population. ...The proportion of Russian families having per capita income below the living minimum by the beginning of 1993 was about 32%". [3].

Parallel to the drop of living standards of the major part of Russia's population, lowering of life quality is observed. This is demonstrated, in particular by such trends having a tragic shade as mortality rates exceeding birth rates, reduction of the average life span and absolute diminution of Russia's population - by 300,000 persons in 1993. [4]. While in the 50's in Russia 2.5-2.8 mln. children were born, in 1991 - 1.8 mln., 1992 - 1.6 mln., in 1993 - only 1.4 mln. babies. Since 1988 reduction of life expectancy began which is still continuing now. An especially abrupt drop of this indicator was noticed in 1993 - by 3 years for men and 1.1 year - for women. During many years the life expectancy in Russia was the lowest among economically developed countries - the last place in Europe for men and one of the lowermost - for women. According to recent data, an average life span in 1992-1993 was 59 years for men and 72.7 years for women. [5].

The growth of mortality in Russia from unnatural reasons was caused by aggravation of social tension, interethnic conflicts, growth of wear of basic production facilities, weakening of all forms of discipline, impaired quality of foodstuffs, ecological and technological disasters.

Suffice it to mention that at the present time the demand of the population and public health authorities for medical preparations of domestic manufacture is satisfied only by 50%. The wear of production facilities at pharmaceutical industry enterprises reached 60%. The on-line plants have not been subjected to any modernization or re-equipment. The starting up of new capacities in 1993 reduced by 3.6 times as compared to 1985. Freely convertible currency is spent not for the development of pharmaceutical industry but for purchases of ready-made pharmaceuticals. As a result, the crisis in pharmaceuticals is still felt.

Without greater investments in public health the death rates will be growing further and the health of Russian nation could be brought to normal only after several generations.

It is quite clear that such situation does not contribute to the growth of social optimism in Russia's population and engenders emigration moods in a certain part of it. Coupled with insufficient scale of housing, poor dwelling conditions, low level of medical care, sky-rocketing prices for foodstuffs, consumer goods, all kinds of services including public transport, house renting, gas, electricity, post and other communications, etc., this desperate situation is a strong motive force for emigration in general. In the case of scientists and engineers, other specialists it is aggravated by the crisis in their professional sphere - science and technology.

At the present stage of development of Russian society the domestic science is in a very bad state. It is quite clear, of course, that many reasons for this are outside the R&D sphere, but some of them relate to science itself which could not adapt to the shaping market conditions and withstand the blows dealt on it by the changed political and socioeconomic situation.

The first such blow which resembled a sudden and instant forced emigration was dealt by the breakup of the Soviet Union when thousands researchers and specialists found themselves overnight in the "near abroad" as nationals and residents of newly foreign states. This dramatic event destroyed the integrity of the R&D complex and resulted in great structural disproportions in it. Suffice it to say that nearly one third of previously single Soviet scientific and technological potential was alienated from Russia without any preliminary preparation. As a result, Russia became partly or in some cases fully deprived of the possibility of carrying out research in many areas of science and technology.

For example, in electrical engineering industry, the research centers for transformer building, small electric machines are in the Ukraine and Lithuania. In chemical and petroleum engineering industries 19 research institutes and design offices remained outside Russia. In machine-tool industry nearly 20 research centers are in the same position. In biology and mechanical engineering only 50-60% of the research potential of the former USSR were left in Russia. [6]. A similar or even worse situation is in other areas of science and technology. Whole areas of research became void in vitally important spheres of Russian economy. In particular, by the present moment Russia fully lost such scientific disciplines as:

- soil protection from water and wind erosion;
- ecological aspects of water-land amelioration;
- regaining soil fertility.

In some areas the losses cannot be compensated in the foreseeable future, since the creation of even a small efficient research team
takes 6-9 years and for establishment of the lost R&D organization
decades were required.

By and large, according to some estimates, Russia's own scientific efforts can meet only 44% of the national economy's needs,
while its capability of developing and adopting novel equipment
and technologies fell by 60-70%. [7]. This condemns some sectors of
the economy to a growing lagging behind industrially developed nations and, hence, loss of productivity, efficiency and competitiveness in the world markets.

It should be noted that the unexpected and unprepared breakup
of the Soviet Union resulted not only in origination of the above-
mentioned structural deformations. An equally detrimental was an
abrupt shrinkage of the previously single technological space which
occurred after dismissal of the COMECON (Council for Mutual
Economic Assistance) in 1991 and, accordingly, resulted in a substantial liquidation of the East-European technological market in
which up to 20-25% of the world technological exchanges were effected. In addition, the domestic technological market of Russia also
shrunk due to the disintegration of the USSR and the following severe crisis of Russian national economy. As a result, Russia's scientific and technological potential found itself in isolation. Indeed,
R&D projects and programmes of cooperation with ex-COMECON
and ex-Soviet partners were stopped, research and production links
outside and inside Russia were broken, scientific equipment and instruments were either lacking or idle, numerous research teams and
individual specialists faced with the threat of unemployment. This
situation pushed many scientists and specialists to leave the R&D
sphere and go to other sectors of activity, or to emigrate abroad.

Under such circumstances only a close attention on the part of
the country's leadership could discharge the growing tension in the
R&D sphere, to preserve and maintain the scientific-and-technological potential of Russia. But this did not happen either. At the same
time, Russian Academy of Sciences and the RF Ministry of Science
and Technological Policy hold but a passive stand and, except
some fragmentary measures, do not substantially take any persis-

tent practical steps to maintain national R&D potential, do not put attention of the government to the problems of strengthening Russian science and technology, to resolving the "brain drain" problem in particular.

Serious problems are observed now in innovation policy, i.e. reduction to practice of most up-to-date achievements of the world scientific and technological progress. The innovation process in Russia becomes more uncontrollable. The scale of innovative activity is reducing, rates of renovation of the material and technical base of production are declining; level, quality and competitiveness of the manufactured products are lowered, thus resulting in a growing technological and related financial dependence on foreign countries. More clearly shaping is the threat of loss of Russia's national technological invulnerability, its transformation from a scientific super-power as it was previously into a technologically backward and underdeveloped country. This, in turn, is connected with a further aggravation of internal socio-economic and political problems, hindered and delayed integration into the system of international economic relations.

Meanwhile, the Russian society, with rare exceptions, has not yet fully understood the seriousness of the current situation in home science and technology. Categories and stereotypes of the past still prevail in the public consciousness in respect of the role and significance of science and technology, place of intellectuals in socio-economic progress of the nation. This results, to a great extent, to underestimation of the R&D factor, technological security in higher echelons of power (parliament, government), delay in adoption of adequate measures for maintaining and development of Russia's scientific and technological potential.

This can be exemplified by the fact that among nearly 20 anti-crisis programmes made available to the public during recent 2-3 years substantially none incorporates any systematic disclosure of measures for survival of Russian R&D sphere, its preservation and progress. At the present time in this country there is not any comprehensive concept and strategy of national scientific and technological development, no appropriate legal framework and economic mechanism have been created. A very modest part was devoted to science in President's Message to the Federal Assembly, dated February 24, 1994.

As a result, the most important strategic resource for overcoming the current socio-economic crisis, for success of market reforms and reinforcement of international positions of the Russian Federation still remains unclaimed either by the state or by commercial structures, thus allowing a further destructive action of negative trends in national science and technology.

At the same time, US President Bill Clinton declared scientific and technological policy one of the top priority areas of activity of his administration, clearly understanding that it is impossible to retain leading positions of the USA in international political and economic relations without keeping up US leadership in world science and technology. One of his conceptual presentations on this subject is titled "Technology for America's Economic Growth, A New Direction to Build Economic Strength" (February 22, 1993, Washington, D.C.).

At the US Congress hearings are regularly devoted to the problems of US science, technology and innovation, whereas in the RF State Duma the issue of Russia's science was discussed in March 1994 only in connection with the discussion of the RF state budget for 1994. As a result of live debates the State Duma adopted an Ordinance "On the Crisis Situation in Russian Science" (March 25, 1994, No.77-1 GD, Moscow) in which the state of national R&D was characterized as "close to a catastrophe".

Indeed, during several recent years nearly all components of Russian R&D potential are in a deep crisis. First of all, this is noticed in financing. Thus, the share of expenditures for science over the last three years dropped from 3.6% of gross domestic product (GDP) in 1991 to 1.2% in 1992 and to 0.7% in 1993. The same level of funding R&D will be preserved for 1994. According to estimates by the Deputy Chairman of the State Duma Committee for education, culture and science, this money is enough to cover minimal needs of science only by 1[3. [8].

The material-technical and information facilities of science have deteriorated considerably. Purchases of instruments and equipment for research laboratories have virtually ceased, a great portion of scientific installations was stopped, programmes of experimental research were cut. Accordingly, instrument-intensity of scientific labour in Russia (making up slightly over 1% of the US level) has continued to decline. While in the USA the average salary of researchers is twice higher than the average in the national economy, in Russia the proportion is inverse: in the 1-st quarter of 1994 the average salary of a researcher was 65,000-70,000 Rbls. vs. 140,000 on the average in Russia's national economy. [9].

The grave financial position of researchers coupled with the dismissal of scientific schools and research centers, decomposition of the scientific and technological potential of the former Soviet Union, rush conversion of the military-industrial complex (MIC), the related threat of unemployment, etc. have all led to mass erosion of the personnel component of Russia's science. Since 1989 to 1993 the number of employed in science and its servicing reduced by more than 1 mln. persons. During this period Russia's science lost more than 70,000 researchers as a direct "brain drain" abroad (i.e. around 10% of national scientific personnel potential; only from the RAS 17% of specialists emigrated over these years). [10].

Since 1989, more than 30% of scientists and specialists have left the R&D sphere and joined all kinds of administrative and commercial structures. Especially painful is the situation in the scientific-and-technological complex of the MIC. Many of high-skill MIC specialists who failed to get employed in commercial firms and bureaucratic set-ups join the increasing ranks of unemployed intellectuals. A paradox situation is observed when the qualification level of unemployed is higher than that of employed.

Some researchers and experts become the target of criminal groups and for various reasons get involved in illegal activities where their remuneration by far exceeds a standard salary. These activities are, first of all, manufacture and processing of narcotics, forging of strong beverages, foodstuffs, cosmetics, etc. During recent time this list is complemented by development and production of firearms, ammunition, radioactive materials.

Most alarming is the fact that the inflow of talented young people to the R&D sphere drastically decreased during recent years. For example, the number of post-graduate students enrolled in the RAS post-diploma training system reduced during 1989-1993 by 4.4 times. The falling prestige of scientific labour, low potential earnings push young people out to other spheres of activity. Other reasons are reduction of the overall number of secondary-school graduates (because of a severe crisis of Russia's high school system), shortage of expenditures for higher education and training of post-diploma specialists, etc.

International contacts of Russian scientists have reduced dramatically due to a growing deficit of expenditures for trips abroad, a sharp increase of prices for air and railroad tickets, international post, telephone and telefax communications, visa formalities.

All this could not but tell upon the efficiency of intellectual labour of Russian scientists and experts, on the dropping prestige of Russian science in the world community. While in the mid-60's an average index of citation of papers by Soviet scientists in the world literature was by about 1.5 times less than that of Americans, in the beginning of the 90's this gap in favour of the USA increased by nearly 14 times. [11]. "Nauka" Publishing House in 1992 published by 2.5 times less books than in the 1-st quarter of 1991 and about 4 times as less as in 1988. While in the early 80's the former USSR was ahead of USA and Japan in respect of annual registration of inventions, now the volume of national patenting dropped by several times, to say nothing about Russia's foreign patenting which is now less than that of a medium-size American company. Russia's incomes from selling of licenses in the world market is only 2% of respective US earnings. [12].

Deformations in the R&D sphere resulted in aggravation of socio-economic problems. They particularly affected the so-called "naukograds" (science cities) - closed research-and-production settlements subordinated previously to the Ministry of Defence and Ministry of Nuclear Energy. Their number is about 70 and the total population -around 1.5 mln. persons. [13].

To many science cities the cuts of budgetary allocations had dramatic consequences. Teams of researchers that took years to form now break up, unique scientific schools and centers disintegrate, expensive equipment breaks down for lack of proper maintenance, municipal services are in shambles, the routes of supplies and servicing of townships that used to be in a privileged position have been disrupted, with unemployment growing and the best personnel leaving. Some of them prefer to emigrate. This might cause undesirable appearance of nuclear and other military (chemical, biological, etc.) technologies developed in Russia outside its borders, in "hot spots" of the globe and in hands of terrorists, thus threatening international security.

It is quite clear from the foregoing that if resolute radical measures are not taken in the immediate future for preservation of Russia's R&D potential, it might reduce to a size threatening national security of this country. According to the OECD estimates, at the present level of financing, Russia can hardly afford itself to employ more than 300,000 persons in the R&D sphere. [14].

In this connection, the role of external sources of support and development of Russia's scientific and technological potential is substantially increasing, thus necessitating urgent measures to ensure a maximum openness of the Russian society and domestic science in particular to the assistance of the international community, international scientific exchanges.

It is obvious that external aid during the current decade will remain an important factor of maintaining and development of Russia's R&D potential, regulation of the "brain drain" process. Now it amounts to $600 mln. [15] and this money should be used most efficiently so as to improve labour and homelife conditions for Russian scientists and specialists, avoiding social tension between individual scientists and research teams in view of a non-uniform distribution of such aid, and eliminating unreasonable obstacles in the form of unjustified taxes and fees for its acquisition and use.

At the same time, it is necessary to make a full use of Russia's own resources allocated for the R&D sphere. In view of an acute deficit of capital investments, the funds for science should be raised at the expense of regrouping research centers, concentrating research in the most promising areas of science and technology, closing useless, dead-end and duplicating one another areas of R&D, reducing the number of unjustifiably inflated personnel in some scientific institutions, restoring the relations with R&D centers of former Union republics broken as a result of breakup of the USSR.

An important source of the needed money should become a further commercialization of the results of R&D activities. Already now the industrial science in Russia earns, depending on its profile, 30 to 70% of funds required for its maintenance. [16]. It is advisable to make a fuller and better use of such new market forms as innovation funds, commercial investment banks and insurance companies and other institutions specializing in innovation business.

As regards basic research funded mostly by the state, the latest developments bring cautious hopes in respect of stopping the decomposition of Russia's academic science. Since 1994 allocations to the Russian Fund of Basic Research (established in 1992) will amount to 4% of science expenditures out of the RF federal budget compared to 3% in 1993. The minimum salary of the RAS system researchers was increased by 1.9 times in December 1993. [17].

Positive signals of the efforts aiming at breaking the negative trends in the present state of Russian science are, in particular, the Decree of the RF President (September 21, 1993) stipulating material support of scientists employed in budget-funded organizations, increased salaries and bonuses for academic degrees, state stipends to outstanding scholars and talented young researchers; RF Parliament ordinances of 1993 declaring assignment of the land which was in possession of the Academy of Sciences, to the latter, with the right of its free and termless use, as well as prohibition of privatization of scientific institutions of the RAS without permission of the Academy's Praesidium. This positive development can be also exemplified by a recent decree of the RF President (December 1993) establishing Presidential stipends to students and post-graduates of higher educational institutions showing outstanding achievements in learning and research.

Local authorities in many regions of Russia also initiate their own steps for supporting scientific institutions located in their territory in addition to the measures taken by the Federal government. For example, the Government of Moscow in 1993 allocated additional 1.5 bln.Rbls. from the municipal budget to the RAS and set reduced tariffs for communal services and renting of premises in exchange for new technologies obtained by Moscow city from local research institutions of the Academy. [18].

The most serious step towards preservation and further development of Russia's R&D potential was the Ordinance issued by the RF State Duma "On Crisis Situation in Russian Science" (March 1994). It suggests to the RF Government to consider and solve the problems of:

- priority financing of basic and applied research;
- elaboration of a programme of reforming the system of R&D organization and coordination in this country and finding sources, appropriate modes and scale of their financing;
- consideration, by the State Duma, of draft federal laws on science and science policy, on the RAS and sectoral academies of sciences and their research institutions;
- granting tax preferences to research, design and engineering offices, educational institutions in respect of their expenses for financing R&D, technical re-equipment, modernization and renovation of production facilities;
- establishment of a special fund for financing foreign patenting of Russian inventions;
- elaboration of draft laws regulating export of scientific and technological achievements;

- preservation of personnel of the R&D sphere (including the "brain drain" problem);
- support of science cities.

These measures intended to encourage elaboration and implementation of a long-term federal programme of maintaining the R&D potential of Russia within the framework of a state scientific and innovation policy are complemented by an important initiative of the RF Ministry of Science and Technological Policy to present an annual President's Message to the RF Federal Assembly on the state of Russian science, as well as by recent decision of the General Assembly of RAS (March 1994) on measures of reorganization of the Academy and its activity under new market conditions.

All this provides certain grounds for a cautious optimism and hopes for a gradual regaining of the role and significance of science in Russian society, finding its proper stand in the process of its further democratization, implementation of socio-economic market reforms. This, in turn, will enable a positive influence on the reasons, factors and motives of the process of "brain drain" from Russia, optimal regulation of intellectual emigration and migration of Russian scientists and specialists.

The following three scenarios of the development of Russian science and technology seem probable in the foreseeable future (to the end of the 90's).

The first scenario envisages a further realization of the current trends in the R&D development of Russia having in general a limited base of using the nation's own resources for the progress of science and innovation. Possible here are certain alternatives for restructuring of the mechanism of R&D management within the framework of general reforming of the national economy. This is, in particular, the reduction of managerial functions of the RAS and transfer of them to newly appearing sectoral academies (numbering now about 40) which can be regarded as an attempt to maintain the potential of applied and industrial sciences. Also possible is reorganization of the RF Ministry of Science and Technological Policy, delegation of some of its duties to the Ministry of Economy, RF State Committee for Industrial Policy. However, in general this can only decelerate, but not fully stop, the process of disintegration of the domestic R&D potential, further decline of innovation activity. In this respect, the main accent would be placed on the use of external sources of maintaining Russia's R&D potential - international assistance and importation of foreign technology.

The second scenario of scientific and technological development of Russia is defined by appropriate political conditions and might result from a probable defeat of democratic forces and coming of liberal-democratic (in the Russian sense of the word) and national-radical forces to power. In this case it is likely that the process of conversion will be ceased, expenditures for the MIC and its R&D complex will be increased at the sacrifice of spending for civilian science and technology. Such progress of events can also bring about diversion of the world community from Russia and, accordingly, a substantial cut of foreign investments in Russian economy including the R&D sphere, discontinuation of international assistance to Russian science and technology. This, rather pessimistic, scenario can have even more detrimental consequences than the first one, but it is not impossible if the nation's leadership, entire democratic public, including foreign communities, do not take all necessary adequate, resolute and coordinated measures to prevent it from coming true.

A third, optimistic scenario is also possible. According to it, the R&D sphere would obtain a new powerful impetus for its advance, as a result of a positive change of the socio-psychological attitude to science and a proper selection of a strategy of socio-economic development on the basis of scientific and technological progress. This implies adoption of a corresponding comprehensive package of legislative and normative acts, considerable investments, social protection measures within the framework of a strategy of scientific and technological development optimally balancing both domestic (state and private) and external (international assistance and cooperation) resources subject to the needs of transformation of Russian society towards a market economy.

This scenario seems to be somewhat ideal, since for its realization no required political and economic conditions are ripe such as political and economic stability, curbing of inflation, adequate restructuring of the economy, liquidation of the producer's monopolism, strengthening of the privatized sector, development of market competition as a motive force of innovation activity encouraging, in turn, further R&D progress. It is likely that the possibility of realization of this scenario will come at the beginning of the next decade.

It is likely that a real process of development of Russia's R&D sphere would be a sort of combination of the latter and the first scenarios: parallel accomplishment of political and economic stability, gradual accumulation of internal resources for investments in science and innovative activity at an optimal balance of its own and external sources of scientific and technological progress, creation for this of an appropriate legal framework, economic environment and a favourable investment climate.

It is hopeful that Russia will come soon to the necessity of formulation and implementation of a state R&D policy for acceleration and success of the initiated socio-economic transformations, regaining of lost positions in the world science and technology, a closer integration into the world civilization.

2.2. PROFESSIONAL, GEOGRAPHIC AND AGE STRUCTURE OF "BRAIN DRAIN" FROM RUSSIA

An intensive participation of the former Soviet Union republics and countries of Eastern Europe in international migration processes caused by a general political situation in these countries and specific features of their economic development at the present stage engendered a deep concern in the world due to a possible threat of a mass-scale emigration from this region.

Both in Russia and abroad various forecasts of short-run prospects of this phenomenon were made which presented the situation depending on the domestic developments in Russia and the former COMECON in general.

The Polish Ministry of Internal Affairs in 1991 published a forecast according to which, after a full liberalization of the passport-visa formalities and enforcement of the Law on immigration and emigration from the former Soviet Union, during 6-10 years (i.e. up to the year of 2000) 8-10 mln. persons could leave it, including about 4 mln. people in 1993. [1].

According to the forecast by the RF Ministry of Economy also issued in 1991 the number of persons potentially willing to leave the former Soviet republics could reach 1 mln. a year (real figures might be lower - 600,000-700,000 persons a year on the average). The number of science and engineering specialists in this migration flow was evaluated as 20-25%, i.e. 200-250 thousands persons. In total, as many as 1-1.5 mln. of high-skill personnel might leave the former Soviet Union by the end of the decade (by 2000). [2].

The Institute of Comparative Politology, Russian Academy of Sciences (RAS), proposed in 1993 a forecast palliative model of intellectual migration from Russia for the period of 1993-1995. [3]. Possible scenarios of this forecast depend on socio-economic, political, ethnic, criminogenous and other factors of the development of Russian society.

Table 1.

Forecast of probability of "washing-out"
of Russian intellectual potential under different conditions
(1993-1995, thsd. persons)

Scenarios of development	Channels of "brain drain"	
	External	Domestic
Non-controllable	550-600	1,600-2,000
Rigidly controllable	90-100	300 - 350
Intermediate version	400-420	900-1,000

Note: all the above data represent the total sum for the three years.

The first scenario suggests a full disorder in the socio-economic and political development of this country, continuing collapse of its economy, political-and administrative disintegration of Russia, growing criminal situation. This situation can result in a sharp growth of emigration of researchers and technical specialists from Russia.

The second scenario stipulates imposition of a strict state control over the departure of citizens from the country, but with preservation of emigration for ethnic reasons (including illegal exodus).

The third scenario which seems to be the most probable for the short-run period envisages possible attempts of controlling this process by the state by way of improvement of the present conditions of labour and home life of scientists, engineers and other specialists in Russia.

At the present moment it is clear that the above-mentioned forecasts did not come true. At the same time, it is very difficult to carry out a multi-factor and comprehensive analysis of migration flows of scientific and engineering personnel from the ex-USSR, Russia and other republics due to a whole number of organizational and procedural reasons and problems stemming from the absence of a unified informational-and-statistical basis.

The point is in that in the former USSR such system did not exist at all, since due to a very small scale of emigration process (mainly of the ethnic nature) this problem was substantially neglected and excluded from the system of unified state statistics. Individual ministries and agencies of the former USSR dealing with trips abroad in their various forms (RF Ministry of Foreign Affairs, Ministry of Interior, State Committee for Customs Control and the like) took their own monitoring and statistical observation of emigration using their own procedures and substantially incompatible systems of indicators which did not enable a unified state statistical control of migration processes on some common scientific basis corresponding to the principles of analysis of similar phenomena employed in foreign national and international practice.

With the breakup of the USSR and formation of the CIS, liquidation of Union ministries and agencies dealing with this process, in particular the USSR State Committee for Statistics, the situation in this area aggravated, again due to preservation of a ministerial approach to monitoring and processing of the emigration data, as well as in connection with the growth of so-called "internal" emigration of mostly Russian-speaking population from the "near abroad" countries which substantially is not analyzed, especially in respect of scientific and engineering personnel.

This ministerial character of presentation of statistical information, lack of comparable indicators in the sphere of migration explain certain difficulties in retrieval, collection, systematization, processing and interpretation of statistical and factographic material in this section.

After the enforcement, in 1993, of the USSR Law on immigration and emigration (enacted in 1991) the situation slightly improved, on the one hand, and became more complicated, on the other. The Department of Visas and Registrations, RF Ministry of Interior, takes into account only persons going abroad for permanent residence. The questionnaire has only those questions which are necessary for filling a foreign passport. Occupation, profession, nationality (ethnic origin) remain beyond the questionnaire and, hence, outside analysis and studies. Moreover, getting a foreign passport for 5 years and cancellation of exit visa enable many persons going abroad on invitation or via other channels not to come back and try to settle in the host country. Persons who thus stay abroad are substantially out of registration.

Table 2.
Number of citizens of ex-USSR and Russia
emigrating abroad for permanent residence (persons)

USSR, Russia	Years						
	1987	1988	1989	1990	1991	1992	1993
USSR, total	39,129	108,189	234,994	452,262	n.a.	-	-
percent of the total population			0.08	0.16	n.a.	-	-
Russia	9,697	20,705	47,521	103,609	90,036	103,700	114,133
percent of the total population			0.03	0.07	0.06	0.07	0.08
Including countries of destination:							
Bulgaria	409	349	311	290	379	221	268
Hungary	115	132	119	200	133	88	58
Poland	96	105	139	177	209	207	213
Czechoslovakia*	142	156	153	178	151	145	76
Capitalist and developing countries:							
Australia	13	49	65	79	304	800	531
Austria	20	9	15	28	20	12	24
Great Britain	45	30	39	40	37	57	43
Germany	3,866	9,988	21,128	33,753	33,697	62,690	73,003
Greece	87	178	1,831	4,177	2,088	1,855	1,798
Denmark	10	7	10	18	6	12	
Israel	3,523	8,088	21,956	61,022	38,742	21,975	20,558
Spain	45	28	24	66	111	154	41
Italy	73	96	74	77	47	80	215
Canada	27	34	114	179	164	292	663
Norway	6	5	6	14	12	12	21
Netherlands	17	18	16	26	18	14	
Syria	44	12	19	7	10	11	18
USA	235	667	678	2,317	11,016	13,200	14,919
Finland	232	192	265	449	583	450	537
France	94	62	58	53	40	50	78
Switzerland	9	13	23	13	15	5	26
Sweden	93	91	80	106	134	208	270
Other countries, including:							
Cuba	123	144	162	103	77	55	24
Yugoslavia**	53	58	63	103	124	100	30

Note: n.a.   - not available.
        *   - Czechia and Slovakia since January 11, 1993.
        **   - within borders of 1991.

Source: Russian Federation in 1992. Statistical Yearbook, Moscow, 1993, p.109; Data obtained
from RF Ministry of Interior.

Monitoring of labour migration seems to be even more complicated. In 1993 two organizations, namely: Federal Migration Service

of Russian Federation and Department of Labour and Employment of Moscow Government obtained the right to issue licenses to state and private organizations for sending Russian specialists and workers abroad on a contractual basis. Within a very short time more than 110 organizations dealing with recruitment of some categories of specialists for working abroad emerged in this country. [4]. Among them such well-known companies as "Zagrantrud Ltd.", "Tekhnostrojexport" and, on the other hand, such newcomers in the field as "Central Council of Homemate Trade Union", "School of Oriental Combat Arts", etc. This broad dispersion of such recruitment agencies as to their quality, of course, hinders a systematic monitoring of persons going abroad for a temporary stay and can hardly give a true pattern of the process of emigration via this channel.

The most complete data illustrating emigration from Russia, its scale and structure are available from the State Committee of Russian Federation for Statistics and RF Ministry of Interior. However, they take into account only persons leaving their country for a permanent residence abroad. Considerable numbers of persons going abroad for a temporary residence are not included in these figures, while according to some estimates labour migration exceeds so called ethnic emigration (for a permanent residence) by approximately 5 times. [5].

The above data show a clear trend for increasing emigration flows of citizens of the former USSR to "far abroad" countries. The highest growth rates of the departure for permanent residence abroad were characteristic for the period of from 1987 till the beginning of 1991 when more than 800,000 persons left the former USSR. During this period the number of persons went out of the former USSR (without Russia) increased by 11 times, the number of emigrants from Russia increased by 10.7 times. Apart from Russia, a great number of emigrants was observed in the Ukraine, Baltic states and some Central Asian republics. In this manner the "closed society" responded to liberalization of going out of the country. Emigration was of a merely ethnic character and demonstrated the urge of the society for availing itself of the opened opportunity as soon as possible.

Later the rates of departure become lower, but the migration pressure continues to amass the emigration flows. In 1991-1993 about 308,000 persons left Russia for permanent residence abroad which was by 1.7 times higher than during the period of from 1987 to 1990. In 1993 emigration was 114.1 thousand persons vs. 103.7 thsd in 1992, i.e. over one year the increment was 11%.

Who are the emigrants? They represent the most economically active, industrious and work-capable part of the population - approximately 6O%. Among the adults 70% were working. In the total outflow figure the share of children under 18 years was 30% (29.8% - 1992, 30% - 1993); men - 31.6% (1993), women - 38.3 (1993). [6].

Geographic pattern of external migration from Russia (see Table 2) is rather wide and covers nearly all continents. However, the dominating portion of emigrants from Russia go to four main countries of destination. Out of the total number of emigrants who left Russia before 1993, 45% went to Israel, 37% - to Germany, 12 - to the USA, 2% - to Greece. In 1993 these indicators were 18, 64, 13.1 and 2% respectively.

The United States are especially attractive for emigrants from Russia. The flow of those willing to go to that country for permanent residence is steadily growing (see Table 2). During recent years a certain growing trend is shaping in respect of such countries as Australia, Canada, Finland, Sweden and some others.

The flow of emigrants to Israel, Greece and Germany is caused, first of all, by national-ethnic reasons, return to the homeland, or reunification of families. Political, economic and social factors, national conflicts, armed riots occurring in the former Soviet Union also play a great expelling role.

The wave of emigration touched upon all social groups of Russia's population, but mostly upon intelligentsia. This social group is most liable to mobility and searching ways for a better use of their intellectual labour. It suffers more than other categories from social consequences of crisis and a poor state of the present science and higher education, sharp reduction of spending for their development. It is this group of Russia's population that is more subjected to external migration and its diminution is the most sensitive loss for the country.

The International Labour Organization (ILO) recommends that in studies of "brain drain" a group of people be used consisting of professional specialists, technicians and workers with similar occupations which could be conditionally related to the category "white collars" and "blue collars". Basing on this assumption, we can determine quantitative indicators of "brain drain" from Russia up to the year 1992, since prior to this period only such statistical data were available.

While the number of persons left Russia for permanent residence abroad increased in 1991 by 4.5 times compared to 1988, the growth in the category of employees was 5 times, students - 6 times. Employees were 21% of the total number of emigrants in 1988 and 23.4% in 1991. Together with students these figures were equal to 23.5 and 26.8% respectively. Therefore, rates of "brain drain" from Russia prior to 1992 exceeded those of the general flow of emigrants for permanent residents. The greatest number of the category of employees in 1991 went to Israel - 59% (vs. 61.3% in 1988), FRG - 20% (18% in 1988), USA - 15.5% (3.4% in 1988). During the above-mentioned 4-years' period the total outflow to the USA grew by 22 times, to Australia - by 18 times, to FRG - by more than 5 times.

Table 3. Number of persons left Russia for permanent residence abroad in 1988 and 1991 according to countries of destination and social groups of population (According to the data from the Department of Visas and Registrations, RF Ministry of Interior)

Countries	Years	Total*	Including			
			workers	employees	farmers	students
	1988	20,303	3,621	4,261	515	507
Total	1991	90,036	13,625	21,062	3,082	3,136
Countries of	1988	1,340	136	463	4	92
Eastern Europe	1991	1,087	84	299	2	64
Czechoslovakia	1988	157	18	65	0	6
	1991	151	14	56	0	17
Bulgaria	1988	351	58	97	0	28
	1991	351	28	97	0	29
Other East European	1988	832	60	301	4	58
countries	1991	585	42	146	2	18
Capitalist and de-	1988	19,463	3,475	3,798	511	415
veloping countries	1991	88,946	13,541	20,763	3,080	3,072
Israel	1988	8,137	646	2,614	18	217
	1991	40,417	3,603	12,460	15	1,866
Canada	1988	34	0	11	0	1
	1991	165	12	57	0	7

Table 3 (continued)

USA	1988	780	88	148	6	127
	1991	11,046	727	3,258	4	366
France	1988	62	2	14	0	2
	1991	43	4	9	0	2
FRG	1988	9,637	2,651	766	487	141
	1991	33,734	8,479	4,154	3,059	612
Great Britain	1988	30	0	13	0	3
	1991	37	1	14	0	0
Australia	1988	49	6	7	0	2
	1991	304	17	127	0	6
Japan	1988	4	0	1	0	0
	1991	6	0	2	0	0
Other capitalist and developing	1988	1,345	158	315	6	42
countries	1991	3,194	498	652	2	113

Note: * According to data on the number of persons obtained a permit to leave Russia. This index insignificantly differs from that of persons emigrating for permanent residence abroad, since the number of persons refused from emigration does not exceed, as a rule, 2% of the total number of applicants for emigration.

In 1992 new, more detailed statistical groupings were introduced in Russia which make it possible to give a broader analysis of "brain drain" process in Russia and to evaluate its dynamics.

Table 4.
Structure of the flow of emigrants from Russia
according to sectors and countries of destination
(according to data from RF Ministry of Interior)*

Countries	Adult working persons, total	Sectors						
	persons,	1	2	3	4	5	6	7
Total								
1992	58,730	16,164	8,736	4,623	4,572	4,110	1,053	19,472
1993	67,775	19,668	9,813	4,765	5,876	4,180	1,135	22,341

Table 4 (Continued)

Group I countries***								
1992	454	78	3	37	31	13	16	276
1993	355	67	3	17	38	30	9	231
Group II countries****								
1992	58,276	16,086	8,733	4,586	4,541	4,097	1,037	19,196
1993	67,385	19,601	9,810	4,748	5,838	4,150	1,123	22,110
Including:								
Germany								
1992	34,202	10,610	8,455	2,854	2,765	2,246	479	6,793
1993	43,457	13,866	9,358	3,162	3,536	2,508	542	10,485
Israel								
1992	13,972	3,355	171	1,217	1,163	1,299	392	6,375
1993	12,635	3,408	297	1,069	1,116	902	270	5,573
USA								
1992	7,964	1,569	82	341	477	445	138	4,912
1993	9,076	1,804	88	393	939	589	270	4,993
Greece								
1992	848	357	18	107	43	65	6	252
1993	743	258	49	61	74	58	7	236
Australia								
1992	514	83	2	21	50	17	9	332

Note: * More detailed data - see Annex, Table No.
         ** Sectors:
         1. Industry, power engineering, transport, communications, logistics, construction.
         2. Agriculture, forestry, procurement.
         3. Trade, public catering, communal facilities, insurance, management.
         4. Science and public education.
         5. Health, social welfare, physical culture.
         6. Culture and art.
         7. Other activities.

         *** Group I countries: countries of Eastern Europe.
         **** Group II countries: capitalist and developing countries.

The grouping of emigrants according to sectors shows that "brain drain" occurs in all spheres of the national economy. In 1992 from industry, transport, communications 16,100 specialists emigrated, or 14.1 % of the total number of emigrants (or 27.5% in the sectoral aspect, or relative to the number of employed in this particular sector of the economy); from agriculture and forestry - 8,700 persons, or 7.6 and 15%, from trade and public catering - 4,600 specialists or 4.3 and 7.1% respectively.

In 1993 these figures became much higher and were as follows: in industry - 19,700 specialists (17.2 and 29.0%), agriculture - 9,800 persons (8.7 and 14.4%), trade - 4,800 (4.3 and 7.0% respectively).

If a comparison is effected in respect of the number of persons emigrated from respective industries with the total number of employed therein, the percentage of emigrants would not be so dangerous, but the absolute growth of the number of those leaving Russia causes certain concern.

This especially relates to the category of science and higher education. Statistics does not show "brain drain" in the sphere of mere science and technology. The emigrant scholars and engineers, as well as other categories of research people are combined in one category of "science and public education". It is in this category that one can show the number of research personnel of the leading R&D spheres who left Russia for permanent residence abroad. In the total flow of emigrants in 1992 they constituted about 4.0 % or 7.8% in the sectoral aspect; in 1993 - already 5.1 and 8.5% respectively (see Tables 2 and 4).

From the standpoint of some analysts these figures are somewhat overrated. Certain specialists hold that the share of researchers in the total flow of emigrants was not higher than 2%. [7]. According to other estimates, during 1988-1992 about 0.3 to 1.2% of those employed in the leading R&D areas left Russia for permanent residence abroad. [8].

However, these relatively low figures illustrating emigration of scientists and engineers abroad should be regarded in the context of their dynamics. Only in this case it is possible to fully apprehend losses of Russian science and of the scientific-and-technological potential of this country in general. Absolute figures of the exodus of scholars are increasing and their growth rates exceed those of the outflow in general and in individual sectors of the economy. For example, while growth rate of emigration to the USA in 1993 vs. 1992 was 114.4% for all sectors, for science it was 197%; for Germany the figures were 127 and 128%, for Canada - 243 and 520% respectively.

The main flow of emigrants from the sector "science and public education" goes predominantly to the Group II countries, namely: Germany - 60.2% in 1993 (60.5% in 1992), Israel - 19% (1992 - 25.4%), USA - 15.9 (1992 - 10.4%). Scientific and engineering per-

sonnel, as well as representatives of higher and secondary education have a high proportion of emigrants to these countries according to sectors: in 1993 their shares were 8.1%, 8.8, 10.3% respectively for all sectors (see Annex, Table No 2, 3.).

As of the beginning of 1993, about 55,000 engineers emigrated to
Israel from the former Soviet Union republics (which is nearly 2
times greater than their total number in Israel in 1987 - 30,000 persons), as well as 12,000 doctors, 10,000 researchers and persons
with occupations in culture and arts, 22,000 professors and teachers. [9]. Only one third from each of the above-mentioned groups
found jobs according to their professions, but many still remain unemployed. In general, unemployment among emigrants from the Soviet Union in Israel reached 40% compared to 10% among the native
Israeli population. [10].

According to estimates made by Immigration Service of Israel,
the number of Jews willing to emigrate from the former Soviet Union
will be approximately 1 mln. persons in 1995 (with the account of
those who will actually leave the country during this period), thus
increasing the population of Israel by 20%. However, trends of emigration from Russia in 1991-1993 point to a noticeable reduction of
emigration intensity in this direction. The number of emigrants in
1993 lowered to 88,4% vs. 1991 and by nearly 3 times as compared
to 1990. This can be explained by the economic situation in Israel:
lack of dwelling facilities, jobs according to emigrants' occupations,
growing unemployment. That is why, if in Russia and other former
Union republics nothing extraordinary happens, the flow of emigrants to Israel would hardly be increasing at high rates.

The second considerable group of emigrants from Russia are
ethnic Germans. The intensity of emigration to Germany during recent years is steadily increasing and, according to available estimates, about 1 mln. citizens of German origin can leave the CIS
countries.

The scale of this outflow will depend to a great extent on the
situation in the CIS region and on the policy of German government
in the context of aggravation of nationalistic moods in that country.
Meanwhile, emigration of scientists and engineers is far ahead of
other categories of specialists - ethnic Germans.

The governmental circles of Germany think that the best policy
in this area will be a comprehensive economic assistance and support of ethnic Germans in the CIS countries with the view to
improving socio-economic conditions of their life there. The German

government allocates huge money for improving labour and homelife conditions of Russian Germans, signs agreements on "step-by-step restoration of statehood of ethnic Germans" with various states of the CIS. That is why a sort of competition originated among the latter for invitation of Soviet Germans to live in their territories. The Ukraine is ready to accommodate 400,000-500,000 persons and to give them the lands which they habitated before deportation. A special program was proposed for 1 mln. ethnic Germans settled in Kazakhstan. Certain measures are taken to assist Germans of Povolzh'e (Volga region) and Altaj (Southern Siberia) to arrange their settlements. Resettled in Altaj region are also ethnic Germans from the Central Asia and Kazakhstan. Rather sizeable becomes the inflow of ethnic Germans from different regions of the former Soviet Union to Kaliningrad oblast' where Germans used to live before the World War II (the region of the former Koenigsberg). However, no efficient ways for solving this problem were found so far and migration moods among the German population of the former USSR are still very strong.

According to official data available from Greek authorities, by the mid-1991 about 30,000 emigrants of Greek origin from Russia moved to Greece. Among them there are many so-called Pont Greeks - descendants of ancient Hellenians who settled on Northern coast of the Black Sea. The percentage of high-skill specialists and scientists among them is not so high. One of the reasons for this - non-recognition of Soviet higher-school diploma in Greece which forces ex-Soviet specialists to retrain to get the right for appropriate job. About 100,000 former Soviet Greeks are likely to come back home to Russia and other countries of the former Soviet Union.

The most "science-intensive" is emigration to the United States and countries of Western Europe. According to data for 1992, among immigrants to the USA from Russia 33% are persons with higher education and 44% are employees. Over four years (1990-1993) about 4,500 scientists, mainly mathematicians, physicists, programmers, biologists, emigrated to the United States for permanent residence. [11]. For example, during recent 20 years about 50% of US demand for mathematicians was satisfied at the account of immigrants from the former Soviet Union. [12].

Specialists in basic research - theoretical and experimental physics - are not rare among ex-Soviet immigrants to the US campuses and research communities. At the present time there are such research and educational centers in America where whole teams are formed from Russian emigrants and even seminars are held in Russian. More than dozen of full and corresponding members of the Russian Academy of Sciences work now in the USA. [13].

The highest proportion of scientific and engineering specialists immigrated to the USA from the former Soviet Union is represented by engineers - about 80%, the second place is occupied by scientists in the area of natural science - about 10%, then mathematicians (about 8% on the average), and computer specialists (about 2%). [14].

During recent time a noticeable growth is characteristic for emigration of scientists and specialists from Russia to the third world countries. Iran, Iraq are interested in import of scientists in the area of nuclear technology and engineering. South Korea now studies the issue of invitation of up to 1,000 Russian scientists, China is interested in employing Russian professors and lecturers in its universities and institutes.

Characteristic for Western Europe (except Germany) is the contractual form of migration of intellectual labour. For example, in 1992 on contracts 8.9% of Russian scientists working temporarily abroad worked in France, 5.7% - in Great Britain, 5.2% - in Canada, 4.1% - in Japan. [15].

Another geographic zone where ex-Soviet scientists and specialists from East-European countries emigrate and go for temporary work is Latin America. Argentina, Brazil, Venezuela, Uruguay and other countries of the continent show interest in intellectual emigrants from Eastern Europe and CIS. However, many of Latin America countries associate such mass-scale emigration with the condition of its financing, in various forms, by the United States and, especially, by Western Europe.

Argentina declared its ability to host 25,000 emigrants from said countries: 1,000 persons in 1993,, 4,000 - in 1994 and other 20,000 - three years later. This country is interested in accommodation of Russian-speaking population from Baltic states, Byelorussia, Ukraine. In implementation of this immigration program, in the opinion of official circles of Argentina, both donor countries and EU countries from which the immigrant inflow is thus withdrawn to a great extent should participate. For resettlement and accommodation of one newcomer, according to estimates by Argentinian specialists, $20,000-25,000 are required which money should be given by the countries concerned. But up to now none of West-European countries showed its willingness to fund such emigration, whereas

Russia and other CIS countries do not face the problem of over-population, but experience a pressing need in financial resources. [16].

There is another aspect which can hardly push nationals of Eastern Europe and Russia to settle in Argentina. The solution of problems of economic reforms of that country necessitates exploration of desert lands of Patagonia. It was planned to attract emigrants to Argentina and settle them in this area along the banks of numerous rivers for culturing virgin lands, construction of hydropower plants, settlements and cities. Such scenario can hardly attract Russia and its residents facing the same problems.

In Brazil the matter is in attraction of high-skill specialists and scientists from CIS countries for work in local research centers and universities. Initially it was intended to invite up to 10,000 specialists of most diverse disciplines of science and technology and the government was supposed to allocate $100-200 mln. for these purposes. It was stressed then that in doing so the country would save billions dollars owing to expansion of the scale of R&D works and attraction of already trained and experienced high-skill specialists. Despite the fact that this idea was approved at the highest level, its materialization into a federal program failed due to the lack of funds for financing such a large-scale project.

However, Brazil invites, on a growing scale, specialists from Russia and other CIS countries on the basis of temporary contracts signed between such specialists and respective research centers. The matter is settled on the level of individual states of the country. Research centers interested in invitation of a specialist file an application (motivating the necessity of signing a contract with him, disclosing the program of his work, its time limits, etc.) with a special commission under the government of the state. The commission considers the subjects of research from the perspective of development of those scientific areas which are regarded as most important for the state. The commission approves particular proposals and enters into negotiations with Russian specialists through the Embassy of Brazil in Moscow.

Subject to this system which is still valid within the framework of the former agreement on cooperation in culture between Brazil and the USSR, at the present time 6 specialists in mathematics, mechanics and chemistry work in Brazil at the University of Ijui (state Riu-Granzi-pu-Sup); 25 specialists in biomedicine and biotechnology, physics of elemental particles, manufacture of composites will start working at three universities of San-Paulu state. Since 1992 more than 20 specialists in aerospace technology work in the Technological Institute of Aeronautics in San-Jose-dus-Campus, 5 physicists work at the International Center of Physics of condensed matter in Brazil's capital, etc.

The experience of Brazil in invitation of scientists from the CIS is of certain interest, in our opinion, since it helps to solve the problem of "brain drain". There is another argument in favour of expansion of such cooperation. It is less probable that anyone of those went to Latin America countries for a temporary work would stay there forever taking into account a strange climate, different culture, ethnic traditions, etc.

The program of attraction of high-skill specialists from Russia and other countries of the former Soviet Union has been also elaborated in Mexico. In 1993 about 300 scientists and top experts from Russia and Ukraine worked on a contractual basis in its universities and research centers; there was an accord on the arrival of 300-400 persons more. During 1994-1995 their number is intended to bring up to 1,500 persons which will be equivalent to 1[4 of the total R&D personnel of Mexico. The contract is signed for 2 years with subsequent prolongation; salary is $1,500-2,000, i.e. nearly the same as of local specialists. However, the latter unsatisfied with such labour payment want to emigrate to the United States and other countries. A paradoxical situation is observed: emigration of the country's own "brains" is compensated by immigration of less expensive research personnel from Russia and other former Soviet Union republics.

Inviting Russian specialists, Mexicans hope to elevate the level of their science lagging behind Western R&D, despite the available laboratories and other research bases equipped according to the latest requirements, as well as to solve the problem of training research personnel. Most welcomed are specialists in physics, chemistry, mathematics, oceanography; professors and lecturers, i.e. representatives of those areas of knowledge where deficit of qualified personnel is especially felt. [17].

The government of Venezuela also initiated a program for inviting emigrants from countries of CIS and Eastern Europe. In general, this country is capable of accommodating nearly 50,000 emigrants among which a considerable proportion should be represented by high-skill personnel. For attraction of these specialists, beginning with 1992, it was intended to spend about $25 mln. A special preference should be given to chemical engineers (about 250 specialists a year) which are necessary for implementation of the program of oil industry development elaborated by the state petroleum company already in 1991. One of the conditions for invitation of emigrants from CIS countries is the obligation, on their part, to work in Venezuela at least for 2 years.

There are intentions to invite emigrants from CIS and Eastern Europe to such other Latin America countries as Chile, Columbia, Bolivia, Uruguay and others.

Uruguay, for example, elaborates its own mode for attracting specialists and skilled workers from CIS countries. It intends to create "free entrepreneurship" zones in the country with their orientation on CIS states. In a "free zone" opened in Soriano department there is an off-line high-capacity sugar plant built already by the German Democratic Republic. The geographic and preferential economic conditions characteristic for all free entrepreneurial zones enable the output of such quantity of sugar at this plant which can satisfy a considerable share of Russia's demand for sugar. But Uruguay has no appropriate engineers, technicians and workers for functioning of this plant. So, it intends to invite essentially all the required staff of the plant from Russia, to pay round-trip tickets for the personnel, to provide dwelling facilities and open a Russian school. It is also planned to invite specialists for fish-processing factories which will be built in Uruguay free zones, etc. [18].

Therefore, many countries are already in the stage of planning invitation of certain categories of specialists and skilled workers from Russia and other CIS countries to satisfy the domestic needs in such personnel.

As regards immigration of R&D personnel in this context, it would hardly take a great scale and in the foreseeable future it might take form of labour migration, since it is not likely that specialists went to work in Latin America countries from Russia would prefer to stay there forever. The difference in mentalities, national traditions, ethnic cultures, climatic conditions would hardly facilitate assimilation and adaptation to local conditions.

Table 5.
Dynamics of emigration from Russia
according to sectors of national economy and regions*

Regions	Number of emigrants	Sectors **						
	***	1	2	3	4	5	6	7
Total:								
1992	58,730	16,164	8,736	4,623	4,572	4,110	1,053	19,472
1993	67,775	19,668	9,813	4,765	5,876	4,180	1,135	22,841
Moscow								
1992	10,296	7	0	0	2	3	2	10,296
1993	7,891	589	8	152	436	250	120	6,336
Omsk oblast'								
1992	6,043	1,638	1,914	779	543	363	115	691
1993	8,243	3,182	1,796	875	760	359	64	1,207
Altay region								
1992	5,487	1,001	2,554	330	787	251	85	479
1993	5,952	1,064	2,706	477	580	301	82	742
Moscow oblast'								
1992	913	558	12	60	108	97	37	41
1993	898	313	17	51	160	141	87	129
Chelyabinsk oblast'								
1992	3,179	730	47	188	146	677	62	145
1993	1,555	695	30	95	194	501	4	36
Leningrad oblast'								
1992	4,679	1,899	0	378	552	631	153	1,066
1993	6,081	1,519	32	364	816	468	189	2,693
Novosibirsk oblast'								
1992	2,169	720	205	134	235	169	58	433
1993	2,001	633	395	116	249	199	35	374
Sverdlovsk oblast'								
1992	1,331	611	24	92	122	156	28	481
1993	2,756	797	15	89	155	134	47	1,519

Table 5 (continued)

Volgograd oblast'								
1992	1,514	640	514	120	69	86	9	731
1993	3,127	942	841	77	136	113	6	1,012
Krasnodar region								
1992	1,995	681	225	290	72	135	15	155
1993	2,127	1,074	222	296	189	172	25	151
TOTAL, for the above regions:								
1992	37,606	7,785	5,717	2,371	2,636	2,740	564	14,518
1993	40,631	10,808	6,054	2,440	3,675	2,638	659	14,199

Note: * For more detail see Annex, Table No. 4
** Sectors:
1. Industry, energetics, transport, communications, logistics, construction.
2. Agriculture and forestry, procurement.
3. Trade, public catering, communal facilities, insurance, management.
4. Science and public education.
5. Health, social welfare, physical culture.
6. Culture and art.
7. Other activities.

*** Number of emigrants of work-capable age gone abroad for permanent residence.

The geographic structure of external emigration from Russia's regions is also characterized by its concentration within several specific areas of the country. These are, first of all, Moscow, Omsk oblast', Altay region, Leningrad oblast', Novosibirsk, Sverdlovsk, Volgograd oblasts, Krasnodar region. The share of these areas in the total emigration from Russia and in its "science and public education" constituent is rather high. (See Table 5 below).

In the total flow of emigrants from Russia according to sectors of national economy these regions accounted for 64.% in 1992 and 60.0% in 1993. The growth of the number of emigrants was noticed in all sectors, but especially high it was in the category of "Science and public education". For example, for one year only (1992-1993) the number of those leaving the sphere of "science and public education" of Omsk oblast' increased by 40%, that of Leningrad oblast' - by 48%, Moscow oblast' - by 45%, Volgograd oblast' - by 97%, Chelyabinsk oblast' - by 33% and Krasnodar region - by 2.6 times.

However, a more convincing indicator is the share of employed in "science and public education" leaving individual oblasts and regions in the total number of emigrants from these areas. Thus, 10% of emigrants from Altay region in 1993 (14.3% in 1992) - people employed in "science and public education"; from Chelyabinsk oblast' - 12.5% (4/5%) respectively, Novosibirsk oblast' - 12.4% (10.8%), Leningrad oblast' - 13.4% (11.7%), Moscow oblast' - 17.8% ((11.8%). Therefore, in some regions the share of emigrants from the sphere of science and education leaving abroad for permanent residence became close to and in some cases is even higher than the rated average levels of 13-14%.

The outflow of such a considerable number of scientists from Altay and Krasnodar regions, Omsk, Orenburg, Volgograd and Saratov oblasts is also associated with ethnic emigration, since the majority of these areas are places of a compact habitation of Germans, while Krasnodar and Stavropol regions are residence places for Greeks. Emigration from cities of Moscow and Leningrad, from Novosibirsk, Sverdlovsk, Moscow and Leningrad oblasts is caused exclusively by economic and political factors, as well as by a worsening situation in science itself.

The ethnic composition of the emigrants who left Russia for permanent residence abroad in the 2-nd half of 1993 was as follows:

Table 6.
Distribution of persons emigrated from Russia
in the 2-nd half of 1992 by ethnic groups
(persons, data from RF State Committee for Statistics)

Ethnic groups	Countries					
	Total, emigrants	Germany	Israel	USA	Other countries	Country unidentified
TOTAL:	48,900	32,438	8,461	5,449	2,272	360
Including:						
Russians	10,645	5,084	2,392	1,848	1,159	162
Ukrainians	860	445	138	191	72	14
Armenians	255	30	41	137	43	4
Jews	9,734	936	5,371	3,066	225	130
Greeks	507	14	2	3	487	1
Germans	25,540	25,469	13	24	6	28
Other ethnic groups	1,325	400	475	167	266	17
Ethnic origin unidentified	114	60	23	13	14	4

66 S. Simanovsky, M.P. Strepetova and Yu. G. Naido

Emigrants are mainly highly-educated people. Analysis for some recent years shows that among emigrants for permanent residence every third person has a higher education. These figures remain stable over several years already for different regions of Russia. [19].

In the second half of 1993 out of the total number of 27,945 emigrants for permanent residence abroad specialists with higher education were 21%, persons with secondary and vocational education were 24.2%. For Germany these figures were 11.5 and 24.5%, for Israel - 34 and 25.4%, USA - 47.6 and 19.6%, Greece - 18.1 and 29.4%, Australia - 60.9 and 2.7%. (For more detail see Annex, Table No. 5).

As regards professional composition, the same group of emigrants for the 2-nd half of 1992 had the following distribution:

		%
Total, emigrants	35,338	100
Including:		
Scientists	367	1.0
Professors, teachers, tutors	1,701	4.8
Economists, accountants	756	2.2
Medical personnel	1176	3.3
Engineers and technicians	1,932	5.5
Managers of enterprises, organizations and cooperatives	715	2.0
Workers	11,058	31.3
Students	839	2.3
Others	16,794	47.6

`Out of 367 scientists 67 persons left for Germany, 136 - for Israel, 111 - USA, 21 - Australia. Engineers and technicians went to Germany - 736 persons, Israel - 596, USA - 467, Australia - 45 persons. (For more detail see Annex, Table No. 6).

In the external migration a considerable proportion is represented by labour migration which is connected with a temporary work of a migrant abroad. These are students going for education, researchers and specialists leaving their country for training and retraining abroad or invited for work on a contract. The contract system, as a rule, suggests an opportunity for a specialist or a scientist to stay in the host country upon a mutual accord of both sides. For this reason it is regarded as a potential "brain drain". According to the data available from the US National Science Foundation (NSF) during the 70's out of students, scientists and engineers who came to the USA temporarily for education or for a contract work 48% became immigrants, whereas during the 80's this figure increased to 56%. If such percentage is applicable also to Russian intellectuals going abroad for a temporary stay (education or contract work), Russia can lose a great number of its scientific and technological personnel.

As it has been already mentioned above, there are no systematic data on the number of students learning abroad or persons temporarily working there on contracts. But occasional separate data provide a certain outlook of the situation.

In December 1992 the Center of Studies and Statistics of Science, RF Ministry of Science and Technological Policy, together with the Department of Personnel, Russian Academy of Sciences, carried out a study of dynamics of employment in academic science over the period of 1991-1992. According to the data of a poll, as of December 1992, there were 1,701 researchers of the RAS (2.8% of the total number of employed in the Academy) on long-time missions (over 6 months) abroad. The overwhelming number of them (81.5%) had an academic degree. Out of the total number of these persons 60% were under 40 years of age and 86.4% were men. [20].

The major part of these specialists (both on mission and working on a contract) were concentrated in the USA (38.2%), in Germany - 16.2%, France - 8.9%, Great Britain - 5.7%, Canada - 5.2%, Japan - 4.1%. [21].

The maximum number - 42% - of those on missions and working abroad on a contract were specialists of three divisions of the RAS: general physics and astronomy; biochemistry, biophysics and chemistry of physiologically active compounds; general and technical chemistry. If the number of temporarily working abroad is related to the total number of employed at individual divisions of the RAS, the first is the division of mathematics (12%), followed by divisions of biochemistry, biophysics and chemistry of physiologically active compounds (9.2%), nuclear physics (4.9%), general physics and astronomy (4.1%). [22].

Among scientific disciplines broadly affected by emigration, as it is illustrated by the above-given data, ranking first are mathematics and computer sciences, biochemistry and biophysics closely associated with applied biotechnological studies, medical sciences. International character of mathematical "language" and a high demand for programmers from Russia put "brain drain" among them in the first place in the whole category of scientists emigrating from the RAS system - they constitute up to 15-20% of the total flow of emigration in this category. According to the available data, from the former USSR about 40% of top-level physicists-theoreticians and about 12% of high-skill physicists-experimentalists went abroad temporarily or forever.

The pattern of emigration of representatives of other scientific disciplines from the RAS system is illustrated by the following Table.

Emigration of scientists from various basic sciences
for the period 1991-1992
(as percentage of the total number of employed in the RAS
system all over the country in respective areas)

Science	Number of persons went abroad	Including those went for permanent residence
Mathematics	15.0	5.0
General physics	4.8	1.2
Nuclear physics	4.7	0.8
Power engineering	3.1	0.8
Mechanics	3.0	1.2
Informatics	3.0	0.5
Chemistry	3.3	0.9
Biochemistry	9.8	1.7
Biophysics and Physiology	2.2	0.9
Biology	5.8	1.6
Geology	2.2	0.2
Geophysics	2.2	0.2
History	1.2	0.1
Philosophy and political sciences	2.2	0.3
Economics	1.7	0.2
Philology	2.0	0.6

Source: Data available from the RAS Praesidium, 1993.

As regards the age structure of emigration from the RAS system, among employees of academic research institutions who worked abroad on contracts during the 7-years' period of 1985-1991 ranking first are scholars of the "average-age" group (31-45 years old) - 58%, the second are "young-age" scholars - 25%, the third place is occupied by "old-age" scholars (46 years and older) - 17%. If a 5-

year age interval is assumed to be a measurement unit, then the peak of missions abroad on contracts is in the category of scientists aged 31-35 years, i.e. 27%.

The number of scientists and other specialists going abroad on long-term (over 6 months) contracts outside the agreements between academies of sciences and organizations abroad is also growing. Such persons in 1985 numbered only 15, but in 1991 - already 451. In general, over the period of 1985-1991 this category numbered 1,051 scientists among which 487 persons went to the USA, 284 - to FRG, 93 - to France, 68 - to Great Britain, 119 persons - to other countries (for more detail see Annex, Table 7).

In 1993 about 4,000 Russian citizens (among whom 75% were specialists) went abroad via channels of labour migration with the assistance of intermediary (both state and private) organizations, [23] as it is illustrated by the following Table:

Profession	Number of persons gone abroad	Host country
TOTAL:	4,000	
including:		
Bank employees	350	USA, Great Britain
Doctors	40	Africa
Zoo technicians	2	Australia
Lecturers and re-searchers	25	USA
Medical nurses	255	USA, Canada, Germany, Cyprus, Central Africa
Teachers	3	Maroc
Construction specialists	1,538	Germany, Finland, Czechia, Turkey and other countries
Scientists	24	USA, France
Chemists	15	Canada

Among these emigrant specialists 33% had higher education, the remaining - secondary vocational education.

Students and post-graduates also intend to continue their education abroad. According to data from the Department of international exchanges of the Committee for Higher School, RF Ministry of Science, in 1992-1993 the complete course of education abroad only under intergovernmental agreements was followed by 426 students from Russia; in so-called "involved" course of education (one-two semesters) 375 persons participated. However, a considerable portion of Russian universities and institutes have nowadays direct contacts with foreign educational institutions and they effect mutual exchanges with students, post-graduates and professors independently. Furthermore, learning abroad are children of diplomats, other specialists employed by UN organizations and other institutions accredited abroad.

Also available are general estimates of the contract emigration. According to them, in 1992 about 6-7 thousands of researchers went abroad on various contracts (long-term, medium-term and short-term) which constitutes nearly 5% of the number of specialists carrying out R&D in research organization within the RAS system. [24].

Therefore, a growth trend is also observed in the contract emigration which reflects the desire of scholars for international contacts in new forms of mobility with the view to improving their professional skills and knowledge.

However, in the present stage a one-way flow is noticed in Russia for all kinds of emigration of scientists and specialists - mainly emigration from this country to more developed industrial states. This trend was actively shaped during the first years of the perestroika period, it is still continuing at the present time. Retaining of this trend might result in such situation that exchanges in knowledge between Russian and world science would solve scientific problems and technological tasks of more developed countries rather than meet own national interests of Russian science and technology. Exodus of a great number of scholars or even of a small number of the leading representatives of the scientific elite is a loss for the country. This might result in disintegration of scientific schools,, individual efficiently operating research teams, loss of "idea generators" and, eventually, in loss of the intellectual wealth of the nation, since the country becomes deprived of its scientists and engineers working in areas of top priority defining the scientific-and-technological and socio-economic progress of Russian society.

In addition to external migration of intellectual personnel, a growing concern in Russia is caused by so-called "internal brain drain". The outflow of specialists from research organizations, design and engineering centers to administrative and commercial structures is going on at faster rates and dramatically affects the present situation in the domestic science and technology.

In general, during 1986-1992 the number of persons employed in the R&D sphere reduced by 1.1 mln. people, i.e. during this period the drop in employment in science was about 30%. If these data are regarded according to areas of science, the number of employed in academic science reduced over these years by 24.4%, in industrial science - by 30.4%, university science - by 11%. In 1992 the process of "internal brain drain" acquired an avalanche-like character. By the beginning of 1993 the number of persons employed in science and its servicing was 2.1 mln. vs. 2.8 mln. by the beginning of 1992. Such personnel reduction rates are close to critical values and can result in hypermobility. [25].

Reduced is not only the cadre potential of Russian science, but the possibilities for its reproduction, since people who left science do not come back, as a rule; the share of graduates associating their career with research work is also decreasing.

According to the most optimistic forecasts, only 10% of scientists and specialists leaving their job on their own will come back to science. The remaining 90% are direct losses. [26].

Leaving the R&D sphere are, as a rule, young men 25 to 40 years old. The outflow from science occurs against the background of a substantially full cease of inflow of young people in this sphere of activity. For example, according to data of observation of a number of R&D organizations in Moscow, in 1992 only 32 young specialists were hired for work there, which was less than 1% of the total number of scientists and specialists employed in these organizations.

A most illustrative decrease in the inflow of young researchers to science has been noticed in the Russian Academy of Sciences. In 1989 the Academy enrolled 3,500 post-graduate students, in 1991 - already 2,000, 1992 - a little more than 1,000. In 1993 there were less than 800 post-graduate students enrolled in the RAS in all areas of scientific research. Russian science is "getting older". The number of research fellows under 30 years age in the RAS is below 9%. In the country, on the whole, the total number of post-graduate students (in sectoral, college and academic science) is lower than of doctors of science: around 20,000 persons. [27].

The number of students entering higher educational institutions, especially of a technical profile, has declined dramatically. In 1993 there were 195 applications filed per every 100 students' vacancies in general (210 in 1992); out of this, in technical institutions - 120 applications per 100 vacancies. [28].

This is explained, to a great extent, by the critical state of Russian system of higher education and, in the first place, by financing. Since 1970 till 1990 the proportion of funds allocated by the state for education reduced by two times. Only in 1992 the state increased the expenditures to 2.7% of the state budget, but then sharply cut them to 1.7% in 1993. Under such conditions many high-education institutions could find no sufficient money to carry on the learning process on a full scale, to buy necessary equipment, instruments, materials, to pay for heat, communication and communal services, to provide adequate salaries for their professors and lecturers, laboratory personnel, stipends for students and postgraduates.

As a result, the number of students substantially reduced, many young people prefer to go to commerce, trade, other business structures, rather than get a higher education. Russia continues to lower its educational level. Thus, in 1993 there were only 171 students of higher school per 10,000 of the population of Russia - far behind USA, Japan, France and even some Latin America countries. In 1993 out of one thousand persons of the population of Russia only 125 had a higher education and in some regions of this country - even less. In Kemerovo oblast', for example, this figure was only 7. The general trend of a worsening situation in the sphere of education in Russia is illustrated by the following Table.

	1980	1990	1992
Persons graduated from secondary school (thousands)	1,882	1,035	919
Persons graduated from vocational schools and colleges (thousands)	721	637	585
Specialists graduated from higher-education institutions (thousands)	460	401	425
Number of students in higher-education institutions (mln.)	3	2.8	2.6
Number of students of higher institutions per 10,000 of the population (persons)	219	190	178
Number of students of vocational schools and colleges per 10,000 of the population (persons)	190	153	141

Source: "Izvestiya" No.60, March 31, 1994, p.7.

In 1993 academic year 1,780,000 persons graduated from 9-form school. Out of them admitted to 10-form school were 55% or by 10% less than in 1992. 27% of graduates joined vocational colleges. But about 200,000 teenagers remained unemployed; later on additional 130,000 were put to studies at vocational schools, but in total 112,000 young people remained in the street without any job whatsoever. In 1994 academic year 1,780,000 persons left 9-form school and only 50% can enter 10-term school. Out of 856,700 secondary-school graduates higher-education institutions can enroll for a full-time education at the budget expenses only 328,500 students so that nearly half million school graduates can find themselves in the street without profession. [29].

Hence, it is not incidentally that in anticipation of such situation many parents prefer to send their children abroad for obtaining secondary education and vocational training in hope that afterwards they could stay in the host country and find jobs or enter higher school institutions there.

As compared to 1985, the number of students enrolled to engineering and technological professions of higher educational institutions in 1993 reduced from 305,000 persons to 191,900 persons or by 37.2% (for the full-time education form - by 21.1%), for agricultural professions - by 26.3% (9.8%), medical professions - by 20.5% (18.3%).

The proportion of enrollment for engineering and technological professions in 1985-1993 fell from 48 to 35%. In 1993 employed by assignment with educational institutions were 150,000 persons, or 53.4% of all graduates, out of which 62,000 persons were employed on contract with enterprises. In medical, pedagogical and agricultural higher institutions assignments for jobs obtained 2/3 of the graduates. In 1994 it is expected to enroll in higher-education institutions of Russian Federation about 483,000 persons at the account of the federal budget, including 328,500 persons for the full-time education which is by nearly 3% less than enrollment of 1993 academic year. [30].

With such decrease in the number of school graduates and students enrolled in high-education institutions the number of professors and lecturers, as well as other teaching personnel is also reducing.

Over the last three years (1991-1993) 20,000 professors and associate professors left higher-educational institutes and went to administrative bodies, commercial and other structures having nothing in common either with education or with research.

Therefore, there is going on an intensive overflow of the intellectual potential from science to other spheres of activity and branches of the national economy. Especially massive exodus is observed into trade (30% of former scientists), industry (20%), finances (10%). The same story is in the sphere of higher education closely related to science. Over the last three years (1991-1993), for example, more than 3,000 professors and docents of higher school of Russia emigrated for permanent residence abroad.

The "internal migration" from science is caused by a number of socio-economic factors: a considerable difference in labour payment in science compared to other spheres of national economy (in 1991 salary in science was by 7% less than the average for national economy on the whole, in 1992 the difference was already 30%, in 1993 - more than 40%, in the 1-st quarter of 1994 it was below 80,000 roubles compared to 140,000 roubles on the average for national economy [31]); impossibility to realize one's creative potentialities in science under crisis conditions; decreasing employment in the R&D and related spheres, etc. These reasons still remain and, hence, the process of outflow of professionals from Russian science is continuing.

The above analysis allows certain conclusions. Despite deceleration of growth rates of general migration from Russia, "brain drain" is going on and dynamics of this process is rather impressive, thus making the government, parliament and other authorities responsible for the destiny of Russian science and technology thinking twice on the urgent character of the problem and its implications for scientific-and-technological progress of Russia.

Mobility and exchange of scientists is an essential component of the progress in science and technology. But at the present stage the process is unidirectional - intellectuals mostly leave the country. According to the Department of Visas and Registrations, RF Ministry of Interior, the inflow of scientists and specialists into Russia for permanent residence was only 2% of the total outflow from it in 1991. The intellectual immigrants were mainly from Bulgaria, Syria, Jordan, Afganistan and China. The quantity of the immigrant scientists and engineers and their qualitative standards are rather low, so one cannot even mention any compensation effect resulting from immigration of foreign specialists to Russia. [32].

The state of Russian science and general socio-economic situation in this country catalyze the process of migration of scientific and engineering personnel. Geography of intellectual emigration, its structure, types of emigration flows (ethnic or labour emigration) might change, but intellectuals want to go abroad. The growing migration on a contractual basis along with amassing numbers of students going abroad to continue their education there becomes a continuous-action factor encouraging potential emigration.

However, the most decisive factor defining both the scale and structure of intellectual emigration is, in our opinion, the demand of Western countries in R&D specialists and other high-skill personnel, the absorption capacity of their intellectual-labour markets and, hence, their immigration policy.

Beginning with 1991, nearly all countries of Western Europe and the USA adopted rather strict immigration legislation. They stipulate quotation of immigration, invitation of mainly high-skill specialists, reduction of state expenditures for refugees' needs, etc. The countries of Western Europe and the USA, in so doing, want to prevent violation of the socio-economic equilibrium in their societies (especially with small population) where anti-immigration moods originate among the native people.

However, such restrictions are not substantially applicable to scientists and high-skill specialists. But, as it is shown by the latest data on immigration capacity of individual developed and developing countries, these limitations would not be an obstacle for the growth of emigration of specialists from Russia, taking into account its present-day structure. For example, maximum absorption capacity of the USA is 749,000 persons, that of Australia - 113,000, Saudi Arabia - 111,000, Canada - 91,000, Germany - 79,000 (see Annex, Table). [33].

According to data available from International Migration Organization, the West during the coming several years can employ up to 200,000 leading researchers and specialists from Russia.

The need of such country as USA - the main center of attraction of "brains" by the year 2,000 will be about 500,000 jobs necessitating a high level of education and scientific-and-technological training; annually this country will have a deficit of 7,500 specialists with an academic degree in natural and technical sciences, already now the USA badly need hundreds of electronic engineers, programmers, chemical engineers and specialists of some other professions. [34]. A similar situation is observed in Western Europe, in France in particular, where a great deficit in scientists and specialists is expected by the end of this decade.

Therefore, it is possible to determine, in general, further development of emigration of scientific and engineering personnel, its geographic directions. This will be Western Europe, USA, Australia and some developing states. The flow of intellectual emigration to the countries which have been up to now leading in this respect (Germany and Israel) is likely to be reducing, since it has been associated mainly with ethnic emigration.

As regards future character of the structure of emigration, according to expert estimates, favourable accommodation conditions are quite possible for the following scientific professions (rating in %): physicists - 68%, mathematicians - 60%, computer specialists - 46%, programmers- 42%, genetic specialists - 24%, chemists - 23%, biologists - 19%, doctors - 10%, phylologists - 7%, lawyers - 5%, philosophers, sociologists - 3%, economists - 1%. These categories of specialists will be of a growing demand in the West.

The world experience and the current international practice show that for all countries initiating modernization of their national economies, intensification of scientific and technological progress and, especially, reforming the model of their economic development, the invitation of foreign scholars and specialists becomes one of the most decisive factors of accomplishing the set objectives. That is why they try to attract foreign intellectuals, as well as to maintain and develop their own R&D potential. In Russia, however, there is observed an outflow of high-skill intellectual personnel so badly needed in this very tense and critical situation in its national economy.

2.3. INTELLECTUAL IMMIGRATION TO RUSSIA FROM THE FORMER UNION REPUBLICS

The problem of "brain drain" - intellectual emigration - from Russia and other countries of the former USSR is being widely debated now by the world community as one of the most urgent problems taking on a global character. Its discussion has put to the second front the problem which has an equal importance - exodus of Russian-speaking scientific and engineering personnel from the former Union republics to Russia. It seems unreasonable to underestimate the scale and significance of this process, especially for Russia and other countries of the former USSR themselves.

This process became noticeable already by the end of the 80's when a number of republics constituting the USSR still existing at that time started to proclaim and follow the course for "sovereignization and independence" frequently accompanied by the growth of nationalistic moods, origination of interethnic contradictions and confrontation taking in many cases the character of bloodshed conflicts.

With the breakup of the USSR the process under consideration gathered momentum and took a new dimension - a threat of a mass-scale emigration of Russian-speaking scientific and engineering personnel to Russia became a reality, especially in view of the fact that the number of ethnic Russians living outside Russia is over 25 mln. persons. More than 50% of them live in two Slavic republics (Ukraine and Byelorussia) and over 20% in Kazakhstan. In these states civilized laws have been adopted on citizenships and languages and no considerable outflow of Russian-speaking emigrants from them is anticipated.

The remaining part (30%) of ethnic Russians lives in states of Central Asia, Georgia, Azerbaijan and in Baltic states. It is from these very countries that a forced migration of the Russian-speaking population will most probably take place for various reasons. Emigration is expected from Central-Asian republics and some regions of Kazakhstan where islamism gains momentum and aggravates religious and ethnic confrontation and social tension. Legally, the Russian-speaking population is put under most discriminating conditions in Latvia and Estonia and if the situation is not improved, the number of forced emigrants from these countries will be increasing. By the way, the proportion of Russians in the population of the Ukraine is 22.1%, Byelorussia - 13.2%, Kazakhstan - 37.8%, Kyrgyzstan - 28%, Lithuania - 10%, Latvia - 35%, Estonia - 38%. [1].

According to estimates by the All-Russian Center for Public Opinion Studies, about 60% of the Russian-speaking population intend to leave Tadjikistan, 40% want to go to Russia from Azerbaijan, about 20% - from Baltic states, Georgia and Armenia, 10% - from the Ukraine and Byelorussia. [2].

This turn of events has become possible due to the fact that discriminative legislation on citizenship were enacted in many newly independent states in addition to some other factors such as liquidation of former Union ministries and agencies which resulted in closure of a great number of subordinated research, design, and educational institutions, as well as related enterprises.

Conversion of the military production, though in an initial stage at that time, already brought about a substantial reduction of the personnel in the military-industrial complex (MIC), including military-oriented research and design institutions, laboratories, etc. Not a small part of such organizations is, as it is well known, outside Russia and Russian-speaking people (of Russian origin) possessing, as a rule, better education and higher skills prevailed there among those employed at these enterprises. When everybody became out of job, they felt a quite unfriendly attitude towards themselves. In many cases it was preheated artificially so as to "discharge" the tension experienced by the population of substantially all republics of the former Soviet Union due to the hardships caused by the drop of production output, disorder of the entire economic mechanism, total deficit of formerly accessible goods and services.

According to the data available from the governmental commission on operative analysis of the economic situation by the end of 1992 344,200 persons were forced to leave their permanent residence places and immigrate into Russia from the CIS countries. Among them: Russians - 110,700 persons, Armenians - 46,650; Meskheti Turks - 41,700 persons, Azerbaijanians - 8,700; other nationalities - 136,300 persons.

The RF Federal Migration Service reported that during the period of 1992-1993 650,000 to 1,200,00 persons were expected to come to Russia, the number of intellectuals among them being assessed to be 200,000 to 500,000 persons. [3]. Out of them: 300,000-400,000 persons from the Ukraine and Byelorussia, 250,000-550,000 - from the Central Asia and Kazakhstan, 40,000-100,000 - from the Trans-Caucasus and 20,000-25,000 persons - from Baltic states. The share of scientists and specialists among all of them was assessed as 5-10%. [4].

Sociological studies carried out by the Laboratory of Population Migration, Institute of Employment Problems, in June-September, 1991, showed that the total flow of forced migrants had a great proportion of persons with higher education. For example, among the total number of questioned people 20% had a higher education, 64% - high education and 15% - low-educated persons. These indicators vary rather considerably according to ethnic groups. In the Slavic group constituting a major proportion among forced refugees they were 23%, 67 and 10%; in the Armenian group - 26, 62 and 12%, in the group of Meskheti Turks - 1, 42 and 57% respectively. [5].

The distribution in profession-qualification groups also pointed to domination of specialists and high-skill workers. Among all the questioned persons 20% were managers, specialists - 29%, high-skill workers - 39% and non-qualified manpower - 12%. [6].

In ethnic groups these indicators were as follows:

- Slavic group - 24, 30, 34 and 12%;
- Armenians - 20, 40, 32 and 8%;
- Meskheti Turks - 7, 7, 60 and 26%.

The picture is complemented by a professional-and-sectoral distribution of the migrants. Out of the total number of the questioned persons prior to migration 43% were employed in the production sphere, 22% - in culture, science, education, healthcare; 8% - in servicing; 4% - in state management structures and 23% - in other spheres of the national economy. [7].
In ethnic groups the distribution was the following:

- Slavic group - 43, 22, 7, 5, 23;
- Armenian group - 26, 32, 10, 4, 28;
- Meskheti Turks - 80, -, 7 , -, 13.

Therefore, forced migrants have, as a rule, higher educational, professional and qualification levels than the native population of the republics wherefrom they are expelled. Such situation can be explained by the fact that in the R&D and higher-education sphere of the former Soviet Union there was a practice of a planned assignment of graduates and post-graduates to engineer, researcher and professor jobs in Union and autonomous republics. Russians and other Russian-speaking specialists in these republics were, as a rule, the scientific and technical elite; they made a considerable contribution to the progress of local industry, science and culture and were a kind of link between Russia and other republics of the former USSR.
The forced migration is quite a new phenomenon for Russia and lack of experience in resolving this problem creates a complicated socio-economic situation in this country. The refugees and other forced migrants found themselves in a very dramatic position combined with the general economic and political crisis in Russia, unpreparedness of the state to alleviation of problems of this kind.
Despite the fact that Russia, with its relatively branched industry and other sectors of the economy, can absorb a great number of labour force, the deployment and settlement of refugees is effected non-uniformly. In some regions there is an excess of high-skill personnel, while in others - its shortage. Especially difficult situation is

in the case of migrants with a high level of education. Representatives of intellectual labour, in contrast to other groups of professionals, are more successful in finding jobs and adaptation to the local environment, especially under urban conditions, but lack of lodging facilities and difficulties with getting residence permits in Russia become an insurmountable barrier for them. Dwelling becomes one of the most important factors of assimilation for all the migrants, but it is especially critical for representatives of intellectual labour who can find job mainly in big cities possessing an extended network of scientific and technological infrastructure. Lack of dwelling facilities becomes a reason of dissatisfaction, warms up emigration moods and turns such people into potential emigrants.

According to the above-mentioned poll data, 29% of the refugees said that they were ready to go abroad. Among them intelligentsia constituted about 50%, including 42% of high-skill specialists and 8% of managers of all levels. A distinctive feature of many persons willing to emigrate is their entrepreneurial abilities, business activity, industriousness. But an uncertain status of a refugee-migrant does not make it possible to realize these qualities, thus inevitably heightening their emigration moods.

The growing forced emigration of Russian-speaking scientists and engineers to Russia having in many cases the character of a panic flight is pregnant with the most negative consequences.

On the one hand, the outflow of researchers, engineers, professors and teachers from countries of the CIS and Baltia quite noticeably and, very likely, for a long time lowers the professional and qualificational level of the scientific and technological (and even production) potentials of the countries losing such specialists. For example, according to Mr. Medetkhan Sherimkulov, Chairman of the Supreme Soviet of Kyrgyzstan, "with the exodus of Russians the republic loses its engineering and technical personnel, scientists, professors of educational institutions, high-skill workers and farmers". [8]. In Lithuania at the Ignalina nuclear power plant with the exodus of all Russian-origin specialists there is a danger of a great ecological problem of utilization of nuclear wastes, since Russia refused to reprocess them for Lithuania, while the latter has neither specialists nor technology for their burial.

In the final analysis, the threat of a widening technological gap between these countries and Russia, the world community in general becomes real.

This process has another side: an abundant influx of Russian-speaking scientists and specialists into Russia strongly aggravates a very complicated employment situation in its R&D sphere. One should bear in mind the growing trend of unemployment of intellectuals in this country in view of the reasons already mentioned above which becomes even more acute under the pressure of the people expelled from the former Union republics on the local markets of intellectual labour force.

A mass-scale exodus of the Russian-speaking population from countries of the CIS and Baltia to Russia which, as to its volume, already surpassed external emigration from this country brings about many problems which are identical, in their character, to those facing some other countries with a high level of immigration. Moreover, in those countries the situation in this area is substantially easier, because it did not appear overnight, but has been shaping on a certain internationally legal basis and drawing upon a relatively well-developed organizational and economic mechanism. It is effective in relation to both the procedure of departure and accommodation at a new place, finding job and integration of immigrants into the life of a community new for them.

In contrast to this situation, the Russian-speaking population coming to Russia from other countries of the CIS and Baltia (unfortunately, now it is difficult to exclude the possibility of similar intra-Russian immigration flows, for example from Chechnya - Chechen Republic which is an administrative part of the Russian Federation) represents, in a strict sense of the word, not emigrants but refugees deprived of their place of residence, property, job, money for living, legally fixed rights and guarantees of reimbursement, though partial, of the material and moral damages. Hence, it is quite clear that their inflow considerably aggravates the situation in the country which is still very tense and pregnant with possible social outbursts).

However, it should be noted once again that the complex of heavy problems of "brain drain" from the CIS and Baltic states to Russia entailing negative consequences for this country still remains at the periphery of attention of the Russian public, parliament and government. There has not been elaborated so far any comprehensive concept of preservation and rational employment of scientific and engineering personnel of Russia as a whole, to say nothing about Russian-speaking scientists and specialists expelled to Russia from other countries of the CIS and Baltia, likewise an appropriate legal, organizational and economic mechanism of their absorption and integration into the life of Russian society.

It should be noted, however, that some, though fragmented, efforts have been taken in Russia to cope with this "internal migration" problem. In 1992 a special Federal Migration Service (FMS) of the Russian Federation was established to deal with the matters associated with accommodation and employment of newcomers the flow of whom already puts under heavy strain the ability of this small and very poorly funded agency. Thus, instead of expected 110 bln. roubles in 1993 only 43 bln. were allocated to the FMS; a similar situation was in the 1-st quarter of 1994 - only 10 bln. roubles instead of the promised 150 bln. At the same time, the number of immigrants to Russia is steadily growing: only Moscow anticipates an inflow of 10,000-15,000 refugees in 1994 [9], while Russia on the whole could receive up to 6 million refugees in the near future as ethnic Russians and other groups from ex-Soviet republics. [10].

The FMS works all alone, without any appropriate coordination and interaction with other ministries and agencies concerned such as Ministry of Internal Affairs, Federal Employment Service, Ministry of Labour, Committee for Industrial Policy, Ministry of Science and Technological Policy, Committee for Customs Control, etc.

As a result, today no one can give any clear answer to the question how to prevent amassing of the flow of emigration to Russia from other states of the former USSR and how to control this flow, minimizing its painful effects and, moreover, trying to use it to the benefit of Russia. It is likely that the time is ripe to initiate an immediate elaboration and implementation of a comprehensive system of measures for resolving this very urgent and acute problem.

In doing so, one should base on the idea that psychological, social and economic hardships associated with absorption of this category (scientists and specialists) of the immigrating Russian-speaking population have to be substantially counterbalanced by that positive contribution to Russian economy that these people are capable of making on the basis of their intellectual potential. When properly used, it can compensate and (judging from the scale of immigration) even surpass the damage which is done to the national economy of Russia by "brain drain" to the "far abroad".

The possibility of such course of development is proved by the historical experience of emigration to other regions of the world. In particular, ex-Soviet immigrants to Israel have considerably enhanced the professional-and-qualification potential of this country.

Already by the mid-90's this labour force by about 1/3 (at the end-80's - about 1/4; for comparison: now in the USA - 16%) will consist of high-skill specialists, thus enabling an increase of Israel's export by 20% in 1995 owing to the growth in it of the share of high-technology companies where these people are mainly employed from 40% now to 60% in 1995. [11].

Of course, the consequences of the inflow of high-qualification scientific and engineering personnel to the country cannot be measured by economic indicators only. Positive effects of such intellectual immigration are also expressed in a general elevation of the educational and cultural level of the country, in a growth of its scientific-and-technological and economic potential, a greater contribution to the global progress of science and technology, etc. But they can bring a real effect only on condition of elaboration and realization of a rational policy of the state regulation of the process of absorption and assimilation of immigrants in the host country.

How can Russia solve such a problem? It has no adequate experience to this effect. Though, migration to this country and therefrom, of course, took place during the existence of the former Soviet Union. But this was a relatively small-scale and predominantly natural migration for labour reasons. It was caused by a great demand for R&D professions and high-skill specialists, professors and lecturers, and by such motives as the desire to improve one's professional qualification, find a more interesting and highly paid job, easier communication with domestic and foreign colleagues, better socio-cultural environment, etc.

In the former USSR these processes of labour migration of scientific and engineering personnel had a legislative control and regulation. All citizens had equal rights for obtaining education in any of educational institutions and vocational colleges in its territory, for occupying vacant posts and positions in universities and research organizations, in particular by way of a competition announced in the press. To a great extent, especially in the sphere of higher education, this process was quantitatively and qualitatively regulated by the state by way of a planned distribution and sending Russian-speaking graduates, post-graduates and doctorates to pedagogical and research work to Union and autonomous republics.

The law also regulated the resettlement conditions; in particular, while sending a specialist to a new place of residence (work) special guarantees were given in respect of his dwelling conditions. The living standards at a new place were frequently better than in Russia;

there were also broad opportunities for a more effective opening of creative abilities of a specialist, his professional career. It should be noted that by way of "migration injections" republican academies of sciences were formed to a considerable extent, as well as major research centers, well-known educational institutions, industrial and agricultural enterprises which made a noticeable contribution to the scientific-and-technological and socio-economic progress of not only individual republics, but of the Soviet Union as a whole.

With the breakup of the USSR the process of destruction of this system went on and took an irreversible character, despite the attempts of some far-looking leaders of independent states to stop it somehow (for example, the decree of Mr. N.Nazarbaev, President of Kazakhstan, declaring Semipalatinsk nuclear testing ground and Baikonur space complex national research centers). But there are no decrees that can force the Russian-speaking scientific and engineering personnel to live and work where they feel the atmosphere of ethnic hostility and threat to their lives. It is only restoration of the previous socio-ethnic and moral-psychological climate favourable for the Russian-speaking intellectual elite that can provide chances for its further stay in the former Union republics and autonomous ethnic regions of Russia.

But, in view of the present-day realities one should admit that such perspective is a matter of a distant future obviously beyond the end of the current century. Meanwhile, there is a very acute problem of a growing exodus of the Russian-speaking intellectuals from countries of the CIS and Baltia and their absorption and integration into a rather difficult and tense social life in Russia. This problem should be solved by well thought-off, comprehensive and civilized methods.

Since in the former USSR, and in Russia in particular, there was no problem of "internal" intellectual emigration, now Russia has no adequate experience in its solution. That is why it is necessary to attentively study the available international experience of use of foreign "brains" accumulated, for example, by the USA, United Kingdom, Canada, Australia, Israel and other countries.

Immigration practice of Israel deserves a special consideration from the Russian perspective. Absorption of immigrants in this country is a goal of a state policy supported by legal-organizational and economic mechanisms being continuously improved subject to changing circumstances in the immigration sphere. Analysis of these mechanisms shows that their certain components can be used for elaboration of a system of measures for absorption of Russian-language scientific and engineering personnel immigrating to Russia from the countries of the CIS and Baltia.

This system should have the form of a specific state program based on a corresponding concept of the Russian-speaking immigration to Russia. Such a program should include legal, institutional and economic blocks, as well as a system of measures for a social protection and support of the immigrant scientists, specialists and their families. It seems expedient to sign an international agreement between Russia and other countries of the former USSR on a free migration of scientific and engineering personnel, including a special section on the order of immigration of Russian-speaking individuals to Russia, or to include appropriate provisions into interstate agreements on scientific-and-technological cooperation or on ethnic and labour migration.

For the purposes of statistical monitoring it would make sense to include migration of scientific and engineering cadres within the CIS and outside it into the state statistics and, accordingly, to elaborate a corresponding system of indicators, accounting and reporting with due participation of ministries and agencies concerned such as Federal Migration Service, Committee for Customs Control, Federal Employment Service, Ministry of Labour, Ministry of Interior, Committee for industrial Policy, Russian Academy of Sciences, Ministry of Science and Technological Policy, etc.

At the RF Ministry of Science and Technological Policy it could be possible to form a scientific and methodological council for a comprehensive study of migration of scientific and engineering cadres in the CIS in all its political, social and economic aspects. Such study should draw upon an agreed concept and a common programme with participation of all ministries and agencies dealing with matters associated with intellectual migration, as well as of public organizations such as Russian national committee on the "brain drain" problem.

Within the framework of the RF Ministry of Science and Technological policy it could be reasonable to envisage a special Department of migration of scientific and engineering cadres which would coordinate practical measures on solution of this problem in Russia with other ministries, agencies and public organizations. Under this Department an All-Russian Fund for Support of Immigrants which could be formed by contributions from:

- state budgets of the CIS countries from which Russian-speaking intellectuals emigrate to Russia in the form of charges proportional to the number and qualification level of the emigrating personnel and calculated with the view to compensating losses of dwelling facilities, property, jobs, other social benefits (as a part of a total compensation paid to the forced emigrants);
- state budget of Russia;
- contributions of public organizations (such as Union of industrialists and entrepreneurs, Union of joint-stock societies, etc.);
- voluntary contributions of legal entities and physical persons from the CIS countries;
- voluntary contributions and donations by foreign public organizations, legal entities and nationals.

This Fund could provide loans to Russian-speaking scientific and engineering personnel immigrating to Russia for accommodation and welfare for social protection during job seeking and finding, as well as allowances (grants) to immigrants themselves and to enterprises giving them jobs. In parallel, it could be possible to provide a system of a preferential financing and crediting, through banking and other financial institutions (such as innovation and investment funds), of budget-funded research and design organizations employing immigrants, as well as preferential terms of taxation and crediting of non-budget organizations of innovation profile.

At the Department of migration of scientific and engineering personnel of the RF Ministry of Science and Technological Policy it would be desirable to form a data base (register) of cadres of specialists immigrating to Russia with the view to ensure control over their settlement and employment. This data base could be also used by a specially established Labour and Employment Exchange having information on vacancies available in the R&D sphere, educational and industrial activities. On the basis of regional research and training centers it could be possible to establish a system of retraining and professional reorientation of the immigrating Russian-speaking scientists and specialists.

An efficient form of rational utilization of the creative potential of immigrants could become, in particular, industrial parks, "technology nurseries", business-greenhouses, science cities, etc. additionally financed from the above-mentioned Fund for support of immigrants. This relates especially to the problem of employment and support of Russian-speaking students, probationers and post-graduates, scientists and specialists previously sent abroad by CIS countries who cannot come back to their former residence after training and work abroad. The point is in that conditions of work and homelife in the above-mentioned technoparks and similar establishments are most resembling those abroad and the process of adaptation would be less difficult and faster.

It is likely that the above-mentioned and similar measures elaborated in detail in appropriate documents, specific programs and projects could substantially soften the acuity of the problem of intellectual emigration from countries of the CIS and Baltia to Russia and to contribute to the progress of Russian science and technology, to healing of Russia's national economy.

References

Section 2.1

1. "Izvestiya", 29.06.94.
2. Ibid.
3. Ibid.
4. "Rossijskiye Vesti", 06.07.94.
5. "Izvestiya", 29.06.94.
6. "Reforma", No.1, January 1994, p.12.
7. Ibid., p.13.
8. Bulletin No.19, session of the RF State Duma, 18.03.94., pp.31-32.
9. "Nezavisimaya Gazeta" ("Independent Newspaper"), 15.03.94.
10. "Rossijskiye Vesti", 16.02.94.
11. "Rossiya", No.20, May 12-18, 1994, p.7.
12. "Reforma", No.1, January 1994, p.13.
13. "Izvestiya", 28.09.93.
14. "Financial News", No.48, October 1-7, 1993, p.1.
15. Ibid.
16. Bulletin No.19, op.cit., p.32.
17. "Nezavisimaya Gazeta", 15.03.94.
18. "Poisk" ("Search"), No.14. April 8-14, 1994, p.1.

Section 2.2

1. "World Monitor", 1992, No.6.
2. "Argumenty i Fakty" (Arguments & Facts), 1991, No.29, p.5.
3. "Nauka i Biznes" (Science & Business), 1993, No.16, p.10.
4. "Inostranets" (Foreigner), No.7, 23.02.1994, p.8.
5. Migration of Population. Collect. Institute of Socio-Economic Problems of Population, Russian Academy of Sciences, Moscow, 1992, p.159.

6. Calculated according to data available from RF Ministry of Interior.
7. E.F.Nekipelova, L.M.Gokhberg, L.E.Mindeli. Emigration of Scientists: Problems, Real Assessments. Centre for Studies and Statistics of Science, RF Ministry of Science and Technological Policy, Moscow, 1994, p.31.
8. O.A.Ikonnikov. Emigration of Scientific Personnel from Russia. Moscow, 1993, p.33.
9. "Economist", London, October 4, 1991. "Inostranets", 1993, No.11, p.19.
10. "Asia i Afrika Segodnya" (Asia and Africa Today), 1992, No.2, pp.6-8.
11. "Poisk" (Search), No.7, 1994, p.3.
12. EKO, 1991, No.6, p.29.
13. "Segodnya" (Today), 17.02.1994.
14. O.A.Ikonnikov. Op.cit., p.39.
15. E.F.Nekipelova et al. Op.cit., p.34.
16. "Financial Times", 23.01.1992.
17. "Izvestiya", 22.04.1993; "Inostranets", No.18, 1993, p.8.
18. "Financial Times", 21.01. 1992.
19. See "USSR National Economy in 1989", Moscow, 1990, p.45.
20. E.F.Nekipelova et al. Op.cit., p.34.
21. Ibidem.
22. Ibidem.
23. "Inostranets", No.1, 1994, p.7.
24. O.A.Ikonnikov. Op.cit., p.48.
25. "Poisk", No.5, 1993, p.5.
26. Ibidem.
27. "Reforma", January 1994, No.1, p.12.
28. Ibid., p.13.
29. "Izvestiya", June 29, 1994.
30. "Poisk", No.23, 1994, p.3.
31. "Poisk", No.5, 1993, p.3.
32. Bulletin No.19, Session of the State Duma, Federal Assembly of Russian Federation. Moscow. March 18, 1994.
33. O.A.Ikonnikov. Op.cit., p.24.
34. "Poisk", No.11, 1992, p.3.

Section 2.3

1. "Brain Drain from Russia: Problems, Prospects, Ways of Regulation. Report to the UNESCO-ROSTE seminar, Moscow, February 21-23, 1994, p.33.
2. Ibid., p.94.
3. "Rossijskiye Vesti", 16.02.1994, No.27, p.8.
4. "Brain Drain" from Russia: Problems, Prospects, Ways of Regulation. Report to the UNESCO-ROSTE seminar, Moscow, February 21-23, 1994, p.32.
5. Program for migration studies. Former USSR: internal migration and emigration. Russian Academy of Sciences, RAND Corp., USA., Issue I, Moscow, 1992, p.91.
6. Ibid., p.92.
7. Ibid., p.94.
8. "Business World", 22.03.94.
9. "Izvestiya", 26.02.94.
10. "The Moscow Tribune", June 5, 1993, p.6.
11. Russian Economic Journal, No.7, 1992, p.17.

CHAPTER III

"BRAIN DRAIN" FROM FORMER SOVIET BLOCK COUNTRIES AND POSITION OF THE INTERNATIONAL COMMUNITY

3.1. DOMESTIC AND INTERNATIONAL IMPLICATIONS OF "BRAIN DRAIN" FROM COUNTRIES OF CENTRAL AND EASTERN EUROPE

The problem of "brain drain" has become especially urgent for countries of Central and Eastern Europe (CEE) in connection with socio-economic and political reforms initiated there at the end of the 70's. The process of intellectual emigration from these countries obtained an additional impetus due to decomposition of the Council for Mutual Economic Assistance (COMECON) in 1991 and breakup of the USSR, wherefore many countries of the former socialist commonwealth have radically changed the orientation of their external economic and scientific-and-technological relations in favour of the West. Another serious factor of emigration moods among intellectuals of the countries under consideration became a drastic deterioration of conditions of their labour and homelife caused by shaping of market relations, change of forms of ownership adaptation to which in science is especially difficult and painful.

For these reasons, the process of "brain drain" has taken, so to say, two dimensions: the domestic one - exodus of intellectuals to commercial, administrative-bureaucratic and other structures not associated directly with research and educational activities, and the external - leaving abroad for a temporary or permanent work. While the former socialist countries are experiencing negative consequences of a combination of both these dimensions, the West is concerned, primarily with the external aspect of "brain drain" from these countries.

This can be explained by two circumstances of both political and socio-economic character. On the one hand, the fear of a non-controllable proliferation of nuclear and other military technologies and the possibility of its appearance in "hot spots" of the planet and in the hands of international terrorists. On the other hand, a heavy burden of financial and other material expenses associated with absorption of a growing inflow of emigrants facilitated also by liberalization of the rules of exit from the countries of the former USSR and Central and Eastern Europe (first of all from Russia) and with the growth of social tension in the host countries (as it was clearly demonstrated by the known events of violence in respect of immigrants in Germany).

Both East and West turned to be substantially unprepared to the ongoing process of "brain drain". In the former socialist countries it took a chaotic and in some cases even a destructive character which is pregnant with a substantial reduction of the R&D scale, impaired quality and a lower level of research and education in these countries and, eventually, lowering of their intellectual potential.

The parliaments and governments of CEE countries and of the former Soviet Union engaged in finding ways of solution of many other urgent political and socio-economic problems have not yet fully apprehended the critical nature of the problem of "brain drain" and its possible negative effects and, accordingly, have not come to elaboration of nation-wide programs of regulation of this process. The steps taken in this sphere do not reveal any systemic approach, they are of a fragmentary and episodic character, have no appropriate legal and administrative base, are not inscribed into the general context of national socio-economic and scientific-and-technological policies. The countries of the region under consideration have no properly elaborated system of statistical indicators for observation of "brain drain" process, its monitoring, presentation, reporting and carrying out international comparisons on the basis of which it could be possible to make necessary corrections in the strategy of development of national scientific-and-technological potentials.

As a result of a substantial lack of a state policy of regulation of the process of "brain drain" in countries of CCE and the former Soviet Union intellectual emigration has substantially went out of control and all hopes for resolving this problem are set in them for the material and financial assistance of the West.

The West, on its part, has initiated rather active attempts for elaboration and implementation of certain measures in respect of the inflow of intellectual elite from the East at the end of the 80's. By the present time the position of Western countries changed from the practice of forcing certain representatives of scientific intelligentsia of countries of CEE and ex-USSR not to come back home, granting them the status of a political refugee during their stay in the West in business missions and private trips and up to enforcement of a whole number of protective measures in view of an avalanche-like growing inflow of merging emigration streams from East-European region. During recent time in policies of the West in respect of exodus of intellectuals from CEE and former Soviet Union a shift from control of undesirable (for the West) effects of socio-economic and political transformations in these countries in the form of a growing wave of emigration towards a purposeful and persistent influence on its deep reasons, motives and factors.

For this purpose, Western states take efforts for maintaining and supporting national R&D potentials of the countries of the region under consideration directly in them by way of rendering appropriate material and financial assistance in provision of decent conditions for work and homelife of scientists and specialists, retaining them in R&D and production spheres due to preservation of the already available and creation of new jobs, especially for persons released as a result of conversion of military industries of the national economy. On the other hand, certain preferences are introduced in national immigration laws of some Western countries in respect of accommodation of scientific and engineering personnel as compared to other categories of immigrants, a certain mechanism is formed for their simplified and accelerated integration into a new scientific community. Furthermore, Western countries during several recent years concluded a series of bilateral agreements encouraging migration of their intellectuals to the West at the expense of funds raised by the West in the form of various grants, scholarships, stipends and other subsidies.

Today it is possible to mention certain elements of coordination of Western efforts in the field of regulation of "brain drain" from the

East on a multilateral basis, in particular within the framework of international organizations. The degree of such coordination is steadily growing, its forms and methods are continuously improved. They cover a broad spectrum of measures beginning with joint international scientific conferences on analysis of this phenomenon and ending with implementation of particular multilateral programmes and projects of scientific and technological cooperation with states of CEE and the former USSR. As an example, one can mention that in holding various scientific conferences and other forums of scientists and specialists participation of East-European delegates is fully financed by the international organization arranging such forum.

Likewise on the national level, the activity of international organizations is directed first of all to restraining undesirable immigration to Western countries, maintaining employment of East-European scientific and technological personnel at home, creation of appropriate conditions for a temporary work and training in Western research and educational centers.

As it is shown by the already available experience of controlling the process of "brain drain" by Western countries, today it is reduced mainly to limitation of the overflow of immigrants in a mere physical (quantitative) sense. At the same time, with such approach the West still has the opportunity of a substantially unhindered access to the intellectual scientific product created by migrating East-European scientists and specialists and those who work at home at the expense of foreign financial support. In other words, despite the quantitative restriction of "brain drain" it still exists in a qualitative sense, wherefore such mechanism or regulation of this process provides one-sided advantages to the West. Thus the total Western assistance to Russian science (already rendered and promised) now amounts to $600 mln. which is comparable with the state allocations for R&D in Russia from national financial sources. It means that nearly half of the personnel of Russian science, even staying in its own country, is detached from resolving important national economic problems for meeting the interests of development of Western science and technology, and, hence, of Western economy.

Many experts think that one should not oversimplify and unilaterally interpret measures taken by the West for supporting R&D potentials of countries of CEE and the former USSR, despite their apparently positive character and the problem of "technological security" should be put on the agenda, first of all in Russia, to avoid negative effects of "brain drain" to the West and of Western aid to national science. This problem should be solved within the framework of a national concept and strategy of regulation of "brain drain" process as an integral constituent of a unified state scientific-and-technological and socio-economic policy.

3.2. PRACTICE OF REGULATION OF THE "BRAIN DRAIN" PROCESSING COUNTRIES OF CENTRAL AND EASTERN EUROPE

Transformation of political and economic systems in countries of CEE is accompanied by a growing process of emigration of their scientific and engineering personnel. It could be expected that the transition from the command-administrative to a market model of economy goes in parallel to severe organizational and managerial measures with the view to adapting to a market environment by way of orientation of an overgrown academic personnel on the needs of production. The economic and technological gap between West and East had to direct the efforts of scientists and specialists to the solution of problems of the economy, ecology, infrastructure, etc., as well as to apprehension of the role of science and innovations during the transition period.

However, the changes ongoing now in CEE countries are of such acute political character resulting in a sharp drop of production, inflation, growth of unemployment, various conflict and crisis situations that the problems of science are moved to the second line, they are not associated with the general situation and economic environment. Science expenditures are drastically reduced, scientific collectives and schools are disintegrated, the status and social position of scientific and engineering intelligentsia are getting lower thus making it find utilization of its potentialities abroad. This situation is observed now in substantially all countries of Central and Eastern Europe.

In Bulgaria the proportion of science expenditures in the gross domestic product (GDP) reduced in 1992 to 1.95% vs. 3.5% in 1985. Total expenditures for science in the state budget were 1.64% of its spending part in 1992. With the account of hyperinflation since December 1990 till December 1992, expenditures for science in real terms reduced by more than 50%.

During the three years of the transition period the number of employed in science and its servicing reduced by two times - from 83,300 persons to 46,900. The relative share of the employed also decreased from 2.2% in 1990 to 1.7% by the end of 1992. [1].

In Hungary the share of science expenditures as percentage of the GDP in 1991 fell to 1.8% as compared to 2.4% in 1981-1985. The number of employed in the R&D sphere in 1991 was 29,400 persons as compared to 42,300 in 1989, among them scientists were 14,500 persons and specialists - 20,400 persons respectively. [2].

In Poland the share of science expenditures in the GDP in 1990 was 1.9% vs. 2.2% in 1988. The budget expenditures in 1990 were 421.9 bln. zloty, allocations for education were 6,211.8 bln. zl., i.e. 0.2 and 3.6% of the total budget spending. The number of employed in science and its servicing in 1990 was 87, 356 persons vs. 96,736 persons in 1989 and 107,700 persons in 1985. [3].

In Czechoslovakia the scale of R&D has been drastically decreasing since 1989. It was especially noticeable in the production sector of the economy. The state expenditures for science and technology from the budget did not substantially change in absolute terms. The annual gain was within the range of 5%, whereas inflation rates, on an annual basis, were equal, according to official statistics, to 14-17%. [4].

In Romania the situation is nearly the same. The number of employed in the R&D sphere within the period of 1990-1992 reduced by 50% as a result of the process of reorganization of the mechanism of management of scientific and innovation activities. [5].

The crisis state of science and related negative effects such as unemployment among the R&D personnel, low levels of income of scientists, lack of appropriate conditions for self-realization of scholars, etc. produce a strong detrimental influence on the scientific-and-technological strata of the society. Nowadays science does not ensure any noticeable prestige, material well-being, guaranteed employment, possibility of professional career. For an average specialist emigration becomes one of means of professional and social survival. The state and society suffer considerable material losses, national scientific and technological, as well as economic potential in general are lowered, thus providing a certain threat for continuity of generations of scientists and specialists.

It is rather difficult to carry out any reliable quantitative and qualitative analysis of the real process of emigration from countries of CEE. Lack of information, compatible national statistical proce-

dures of monitoring, presentation and reporting, compatible indicators do not enable a clear pattern of the process.

According to some available estimates, since the end of 1981 till
the end of 1991 about 50,000 high-skill specialists left Bulgaria via
different migration channels. The share of researchers and university
professors among them is 15-20%. The professional structure of the
migrant intellectuals is shown in Table 1 below.

Table 1.
Emigrants with higher education from Bulgaria in 1990

Professional groups	Total number,	
	persons	%
T O T A L	23,469	100
economists and specialists		
in agriculture	5,098	21.7
scientists	4,395	18.7
sportsmen	879	3.7
doctors	4,571	19.4
engineers	8,526	36.3

Source: Data of the National Statistical Institute of Bulgaria.

Among the scientists who left the country specialists in molecular biology prevailed (38% of specialists of this profile working in
Bulgaria emigrated), applied cybernetics (14.3%), medical sciences
(9.6%), computer software (2.5%), optics (2%).

Geography of emigration is associated mainly with Germany,
USA, Canada, France, Great Britain. For example, by the beginning
of 1992 28% of Bulgarian microbiologists emigrated to Germany, 5%
- to the USA and Canada, 13% to France, 17% - South Africa;
among medical specialists 25% went to Germany, 17% to the USA
and Canada, 42% - to France, 8% - Great Britain; specialists in optics and precise mechanics: 13% - to Germany, 32% - USA and
Canada, 11% - France, 10% - Great Britain. [6].

Emigrants aged 31-40 years prevail in the outflow of scientific
and engineering personnel from Bulgaria (45% of the total number of
emigrants), ranking second are specialists of 41050 years old (about
50%), i.e. leaving the country forever are scientists and specialists
who are in the most work-capable age categories.

According to the data of the National Statistical Institute and the results of studies carried out by the Centre for studying democracy (CSD), in 1990, 1991, 1992 emigration moods of Bulgarian population were still very strong. The potential mobility remained at the level of 26-28% of the labour-active population of the country. The greatest proportion of potential emigrants are people with higher education. According to the above-mentioned poll by CSD, 15.9% of those willing to emigrate had higher education, 11.5% - high education.

The data available in respect of two Bulgarian Academies: Academy of Sciences and Medical Academy, out of 450 questioned scientists 89% had the intention to leave the country for a long time for work abroad, including 25% in the immediate future, and the remaining 64% - in a distant perspective. [7].

A considerable role in progress of migration mobility of scientists and specialists from Bulgaria was played by the Law on additional requirements to members of the board of research organizations and the Highest Attestation Commission enforced in 1992. It has become known as the Law on decommunization of science. According to its provisions, nobody out of the former Bulgarian communist party apparatus can take and occupy managerial posts in research and educational institutions. This law and reorganization of research institutes initiated in 1992 brought about an "explosion" of "internal" and external emigration from the country. The reorganization touched upon, first of all, research centers related to industry where mass lock-outs and reduction of personnel were effected. These structural changes were carried out chaotically, without taking into consideration long-term objectives of scientific development and, hence, resulted in serious losses in the intellectual potential of the nation.

In Hungary - the most open country of the Eastern block - the process of emigration started a decade earlier - since 1979 and reached its climax in 1988-1989. The emigration curve is now in its maximum and, as it can be judged from certain symptoms, is nearing a certain equilibrium.

According to some estimates, at the present time about 4,200 Hungarian scientists and specialists (or 15% of the total number of researchers in the country) work abroad. This figure, in our opinion, includes also the scientists already working in or invited to foreign countries for a term of three months and longer, i.e. it includes temporary emigrants, wherefore these data seem to be somewhat lowered. However, according to the information of the Hungarian Academy of Sciences, the number of specialists leaving the country for a long-term mission (over three months) was at the level of about 10% during the last three years; the number of engineers and scientists who work abroad for a period of from three months to several years, is equal to 4.7% (1,250 persons).

Intellectual emigrants from Hungary are representatives of natural sciences, medicine. For example, in 1990 out of 331 emigrants 114 persons represented natural sciences, 103 - medicine, social sciences - only 7 persons and agriculture - 10 specialists. [8].

Hungarian experts point to one specific component in the migration process in Hungary which has obtained the name of "cross migration". This term means that intellectuals who live in border countries move to Hungary and continue to work there according to their professions. For example, during several recent years about 1,500 physicists from countries neighbours of Hungary moved into it and are working there now according to their previous occupation. From the point of view of the Hungarian side, these problems are easy to regulate by way of signing appropriate agreements with neighbour countries officially allowing exchanges of specialists and their coming back home freely upon completion of their job.

Poland also suffers great losses from emigration of scientific and engineering personnel. During the 80's this country was left by 19,800 engineers, 11,500 doctors and nurses, 8,800 scientists. According to calculations by Polish experts, about 10% of the total scientific personnel emigrated from Poland forever for work abroad.

Observations carried out in 1,003 scientific organizations with the total staff of 28,500 researchers give more detailed information on the scale, professional structure, geographic directions of intellectual emigration from Poland.

Table 2.
Number of scientists emigrated from Poland during 1981-1991

Countries	Total, for the period, %	Years		
		1981-1984	1985-1988	1989-1991
Total number of emigrants, persons	2,706	1,208	924	574
USA	33.8	33.4	32.3	36.6
Germany	23.4	20.9	27.2	22.6
Canada	13.6	15.4	12.9	10.8
France	4.9	4.6	4.6	5.7
Great Britain	3.8	3.4	3.6	5.0
Other European countries	11.8	13.2	11.1	9.8
Other non-European countries	8.8	9.1	8.0	9.4

Source: "Brain Drain" in Poland. University of Warsaw, European Institute for Regional and Local Development, Warsaw, 1992, p.52.

Over the above-specified period 2,706 scientists left Poland, the majority of them went to the USA - 33.8%, Germany - 23.4%, Canada - 13.6%. These three countries have a steady attractiveness for Polish scientists and researchers. Countries of European Union account for a considerably lesser share.

Professional structure of the emigrant flow is as follows.

Table 3.
Professional occupations of Polish intellectual emigrants
(1981-1991, persons)

Science discipline	Number of emigrants, persons	Proportion of working in their professions abroad %
Biology	292	40.1
Physics	224	30.8
Chemistry	163	27.0
Mathematics and informatics	167	23.4
Natural sciences and geography	119	21.8
Engineering and technological sciences	791	21.1
Humanitarian sciences	212	18.4
Economics and management	79	17.7
Agriculture	68	16.2
Medicine	441	15.2
Social sciences and law	148	13.5

Source: "Brain Drain" in Poland..., Opt.cit., p.58.

Representatives of engineering and technological sciences, medical personnel, physicists and biologists prevail in the general flow of intellectual emigrants. The age distribution of Polish emigrants has a higher proportion of young and middle-age specialists falling in the categories of 25-30 and 31-45 years old.

Polish experts note that the process of intellectual emigration is still continuing. It is also mentioned that Polish students tend to get a relatively inexpensive academic education at home for a subsequent successful employment in the West.

Emigration of intellectual professionals is an urgent problem for Romania. Observation of 222 research institutes with the total number of employed researchers of 40,000 persons showed that after 1989 from these organizations 446 specialists left the country, their professional distribution is given in Table 4.

Table 4. Number of scientists emigrated from Romania after 1989

Research field	Number of emigrants with higher education, persons	Percentage of emigrants with higher education, %
Power engineering	25	8.7
Raw materials (coal, oil, gas, minerals)	19	0.7
Machine-building	188	2.0
Electrical engineering, electronics, precise mechanics	54	0.9
Chemistry	18	0.2
Metallurgy	3	0.15
Forestry, pulp-and-paper industry	14	1.5
Light industry	7	0.6
Transport	23	2.0
Agriculture, food industry	8	0.2
Construction, seismic construction, building materials	60	4.0
Medicine	25	0.9
Others	2	0.4
TOTAL:	446	1.1

Source: Studies of the Ministry of Development and Technology of Romania, 1993.

From the above-listed areas of R&D of Romania 446 researchers emigrated which was equal to 1.1% of the R&D potential of these spheres. However, in other spheres of scientific activity such as informatics, mathematics, physics, etc. the number of emigrants is even higher - up to 5% of the total number of employed. [9].

In Hungary the number of intellectuals staying abroad for a temporary (for a period of longer than three months' duration) or permanent work relative to the total number of employed in the R&D sphere is even higher. It was around 10% in 1986, reached its maximum of 17.5% in 1987, decreased to 14% in 1988 and fluctuated around 10% during 1989-1992, thus constituting an average figure of about 12% for the period of 1987-1992. The number of those working abroad was divided by half-and-half between employees and scholarship-holders. A slightly better situation with "brain drain" is in research institutions of the Hungarian Academy of sciences. Thus, according to data provided by the National Statistical Office of Hungary, out of the total number of scientists and engineers employed in the system of the Academy 4.7% (or 11,250 persons) were staying abroad for a period longer than three months in 1991. Within thus figure, R&D employees and scholarship-holders shared alike. [10].

In Czech Academy of Sciences a sharp drop in the number of employed occurred during the period of 1989 to 1993 from 13,800 persons to 6,500 persons, including decrease of the number of researchers from 4,100 to 3,200 persons. In 1992 740 researchers left the Academy, in 1993 - 150. However, there is no information as to the proportions in which those who left science in the Academy were divided into the "internal" and "external migration".

The problems of internal migration or change of the activity area in home country are to some extent rather typical for all countries of Central and Eastern Europe. The intellectuals escape to commercial, bureaucratic and administrative structures, services and other areas having sometimes nothing in common with research and pedagogical occupations. In Poland, Romania and Hungary the "internal" migration from science is superior, as to its scale, to the external migration and considerably affects the state and prospects of the development of the R&D potential of these countries towards its deterioration. In 1991 the "internal" migration in Poland was 15.1% of the total number of employed in the R&D sphere (external migration - 9.5%), in Romania - even 30% (external - 5%).

The "internal" and "external" migration of scientific and engineering personnel in CEE countries is caused by numerous factors described in detail hereinbelow, but two of them worth mentioning here as the most decisive ones. These are a considerable difference in labour remuneration and impossibility of realization of one's creative abilities in his own country, as well as a growing unemployment among people of a creative labour.

The situation in emigration now shaped in CEE countries entails, though to a different extent, substantial material and social-and-psychological damage to them. Its negative repercussions should be reconsidered in a broader and long-term context. Weakening of the national R&D potential as a result of loss of professionals, lowering of creative capacities of the intellectual elite might result in the decline of the scientific and technological level of national development, to deprive the nation of its intellectual elite indispensable for keeping up the spirit of creativity and entrepreneurship in the society, maintaining its balanced social structure.

CEE countries are facing a difficult problem. Since they want to be integrated into the economic and technological space of the OECD states, despite all the difficulties encountered along this way, they have to create appropriate conditions for the formation of an open and viable scientific community. That is why preservation of the already accumulated R&D potential, modification and modernization of its structure, elaboration of a well-thought scientific and innovation policy must become top-priority objectives of these countries. A scientific and technological policy based on a comprehensive approach should take into consideration the role of science as a motor of socio-economic progress of the nation.

CEE countries have to solve the problem of "brain drain" under very tense conditions. In the present stage of transition towards a market model of economic development a very difficult situation is observed in substantially all of them. The state does not possess sufficient resources for maintenance of the overgrown state sector of science. At the same time, higher educational institutions and, especially, industry undergoing modernization are experiencing an acute deficit in specialists of modern professions.

All countries of CEE are interested in attraction of scientists and highly qualified professionals into industry who could make a direct contribution to restructuring and progress of national production. Furthermore, the reduction of the state sector of science might provide an opportunity of moving a great number of scientists and specialists for work at higher educational institutions which are also faced with a growing deficit in modern equipment and specialists possessing up-to-date knowledge and expertise.

An inter-sectoral mobility can become an important factor re-straining "brain drain". Redeployment of big groups of specialists from one sphere of activity into another can preserve qualified personnel for the country, reduce unemployment, help in solving the problem of training and education. However, employment of the released personnel is associated with the necessity of its retraining which requires organization of special professional courses. At the same time, during the transition period when a clear concept of the development of national economy, industry, science and technology is lacking, it is very difficult to elaborate a proper structure of re-training and reprofilization of scientific and technological personnel.

Substantially all countries of CEE have to solve the problems of regaining prestige of scientific labour, creation of normal working conditions for scientists, elimination of the gap in labour payment in the R&D sphere and in other sectors of national economy, overcoming obstacles in the way of scientific research and innovation. According to estimates of some Polish experts, at the present time an average annual salary of researchers and university professors in Poland is equivalent to $2,500; with all bonuses and benefits it can be as high as $5,000, whereas in the USA an annual salary of a specialist of the same level can vary from $70,000 to $120,000. [11]. If such situation in Poland prevails for several years more, according to the available forecasts, one could envisage discontinuation of existence of Polish science and universities and impossibility of reproduction of high-qualification personnel.

A great contribution to resolving these problems can be made by extending contacts with previously emigrated or recently departed scientists and specialists. In some cases their homeland can count on their coming back home or on temporary returns which is also an efficient channel for the "reverse transfer" of knowledge and expertise obtained by them abroad.

Up to the present moment no special programs for regulation of "brain drain" from CEE countries were elaborated. However, this problem is touched upon in general programs worked out by international organizations and European communities on request from individual CEE countries. For example, the OECD prepared a report on scientific and technological policy of the former Czechoslovakia within the framework of the program "Partners in the Transition period". The recommendations and conclusions of the report are employed now by the Ministry of Education and Science of the Slovak Republic in elaboration of the national scientific-and-technological policy. Certain specific proposals are given in the fundamental report "Mobility of Scientists and Specialists between OECD Countries and Countries of Central and Eastern Europe" (Vienna, February 1993) which also suggests ways and means for resolving this problem in its various aspects.

According to recommendations of a number of such documents and several initiatives of their own, CEE countries tend to minimize the negative effects of the "brain drain" phenomenon and improve the mechanism of its control and regulation.

The most extensive activity in this direction is demonstrated by Hungary which follows a policy of restraining emigration of scientific personnel and encouraging their coming back home with the view to reintegrating into the national scientific community.

The government has formulated the task and undertaken a number of administrative measures for initiating contacts with Hungarian scientists who left the country many years ago in order to involve them in scientific life of their homeland.

Several years ago a system of financial support of scientific personnel was established in Hungary. Its main component is the fund of basic research. Being an employee of a foreign (say, American) research center, a specialist can get a grant and come to his homeland to make a respective work as a contractor from overseas. Such return has a certain psychological shade and moral stimuli. The Academy of Science of Hungary offers to prominent "American Hungarians" prestigious posts, beneficial contracts, high salaries, invites to deliver lectures as visiting professors in universities, summer schools; it also practices exchanges of scientists and specialists.

They are also offered to become members of learned councils of research institutes and universities, or specialized science committees at Hungarian Academy of Sciences, to participate in activities of managerial bodies of scientific societies.

With the assistance from Chicago University the Hungarian Academy of sciences issues a daily newspaper for Hungarian scientists working in the USA which is distributed via electronic post and computer network. In this manner Hungarian scientists are not separated from their homeland, they feel its attention to them and they communicate with each other and with Hungarian colleagues through this newspaper.

While maintaining relations with emigrated professors and lecturers the Hungarian side asks many of them to receive Hungarian post-graduates for training. If even a part of them would prefer to stay abroad, in the USA in particular, the remaining young scholars would come home having made certain connections and acquired scientific knowledge and expertise useful for maintaining international contacts and carrying out further research at their homeland. According to the available data, about 800 Hungarian post-graduate students in the USA communicate with each other through an electronic information network, thus providing conditions for a mutual assistance, continuous contacts, exchange of news and scientific information.

Hungary carries out a purposeful policy of cooperation with foreign partners in organization and hosting of scientific events. For example, during 1986-1992 Hungarian Academy of Sciences together with international organizations arranged about 800 international scientific events out of which about 33% were held in Hungary. This enabled national research centers to get acquainted with international experience and progress in various research areas reported at respective conferences, symposia and other scientific forums. [12].

Enlarging its participation in internationalization of science and innovation via the channels of cooperation with European Union (EU), Hungary joined such international programs as EUREKA, PHARE, TEMPUS, COST and others. It also has signed cooperation agreements with such international research centers as CERN, ESA, EMBO and the like, foundations as ESF, etc. Hungarian experts find that those specialists who are engaged in international scientific activity within R&D programs or joint-venture projects and spend their time partly abroad, partly at home individually or in cooperation with a visiting foreign partner are much less subjected to the negative effects of "brain drain".

Such practices of Hungarian authorities and research organizations start to bear fruit in controlling the process of "brain drain" from the country. At present, a certain phenomenon of remigration is observed in Hungary. Researchers having worked 5 to 6 years abroad are coming home either because their research project has been completed, or they have not found an adequate support for continuation of their research work, or for some other reasons including the possibility of obtaining better job and homelife conditions in Hungary.

Romania solves its problems of "brain drain" on a broader state level within the framework of a national policy of regulation of this process. During the ongoing restructuring of its national economy

Romania granted independence to all its research centers in functioning and management, establishing direct contacts with R&D organizations both in the country and abroad, elaboration of scientific programs and projects, educational training courses, exchanges of specialists and professors between research organizations and universities.

This activity complements a number of agreements and contracts signed on the governmental level. Subject to various state programs (both national and international), over the period of 1990-1992 more than 150 Rumanian professors and lecturers were teaching full or partial training cycles abroad, mainly in Western Europe; 285 scientists were in short-term missions in Germany, Spain, France and Italy within the framework of TEMPUS program, more than 50 students continued their education abroad under students' exchange programs. [13].

Besides, Romania provides a number of various stipends intended for ethnic Romanians (students, doctorates, probationers, post-graduates, etc.) living abroad for education or training at Rumanian research and educational institutions,

I. MOLDAVIA

1. Since 1990 the government of Romania offered stipends for education, doctorates and training of ethnic Romanians from Republic of Moldova:

1990-1991	students	1,290 persons
	doctorates	140 persons
	training courses	15 persons
1991-1992	students	650 persons
	doctorates	200 persons
	training courses	100 monthly stipends
1992-1993	students	1,000 persons
	doctorates	200 persons
	training courses	100 monthly stipends

2. At the present time in Romania there are on such stipends:

university education	3,200 ethnic Romanian students from Moldova;
doctorates	360 ethnic Romanians from Moldova;
training courses	100 monthly stipends for ethnic Romanians from Moldova annually.

II. UKRAINE

1. Since 1991 the government of Romania offered stipends and scholarships for students, doctorates and trainees of Romanian ethnic origin from the Ukraine:

	1991-1992
students	200 persons
doctorates	20 persons
training courses	40 monthly stipends

2. At the present time in Romania there are on such stipends:

university education	315 students from the Ukraine;
doctorates	4 persons - ethnic Romanians;
training courses	12 monthly stipends.

During 1991-1992 young people from the Ukraine came to Romania on the basis of competition and subject to the documents prepared by the Ministry of Science and Education of the Republic of Moldova, since there was no agreement on cooperation between the Ministry of education of the Ukraine and the government of Romania. In 1992-1993 young ethnic Romanians from the Ukraine were chosen and officially sent to Romania by the Ministry of Education of the Ukraine under the Protocol on Cooperation signed by respective national authorities of both states in August 1992.

III. OTHER COUNTRIES

For the education year 1992/1993 the government of Romania offered stipends and vacancies for education at one's own account on a currency-free basis to ethnic Romanians from neighbouring countries:

Albania	60 stipends and 10 vacancies at one's own expenses;
Bulgaria	20 stipends and 60 vacancies --- " ---;
Greece	15 stipends and 20 vacancies --- " ---;
Yugoslavia	60 stipends and 150 vacancies --- " ---;
Hungary	50 stipends and 75 vacancies --- " ---.

Some stipendiates have already started their studies in Romania. The process of selection of candidates is effected with participation of Romanian Embassies in chosen countries.

By granting stipends to young ethnic Romanians from foreign countries, Romania enlarges the area of mobility of high-skill personnel for the future and helps to solve the problem of obtaining higher education and academic degrees by representatives of Romanian ethnic minorities in neighbouring countries, thus contributing to relaxation of social and ethnic tension, restraining the scale of exodus of "Romanian brains" from them.

For a financial aid to national science, a special foundation has been established in Romania. It will be formed by charges from the turnover of commercial companies of Romania (1%) in favour of financing basic research which is intended to be an essential support of this area of science in addition to the state budget.

Poland takes numerous measures to keep specialists, especially of rare professions, at home. For example, upon leaving abroad conditions of return of specialists are included into provisions of appropriate contracts. Among such provisions - charging a portion of the earnings abroad (about 25%) in favour of the institute that sent a specialist for a mission abroad, limitation of the period of staying abroad (most frequently to 5 years) and others.

Poland widely uses mobility of scientists and specialists in its interests. As compared to other former socialist countries those were Poland and Hungary that enjoyed far broader freedom and opportunities for their nationals to work abroad. Polish professors invited for work abroad or researchers who obtained foreign grants started their work abroad on a mass scale even since 1970.

At the present time the country intends to regain contacts with specialists who left Poland long ago in order to involve their knowledge and expertise in the process of reforming national economy and democratization of the Polish society.

Despite different character of measures taken by each individual country of Central and Eastern Europe in respect of control and regulation of the "brain drain" process and preservation of their R&D potentials, they set great hopes for the assistance and support in this area from countries of the OECD and other industrially developed states of the West.

3.3. RESPONSE OF INDIVIDUAL FOREIGN COUNTRIES TO "BRAIN DRAIN" FROM FORMER SOVIET BLOCK COUNTRIES

The position of states of the West in respect of "brain drain" from former socialist countries is not unambiguous, since it is shaped under the influence of numerous political, social and economic factors frequently acting in different directions. Some of these factors dictate the necessity of a liberal attitude of Western countries to the problem of mobility of scientific and engineering personnel both domestic and foreign. Other factors force these countries to hold an opposite position. In general, one should base on the assumption that the resultant vector of these factors defining the position of this or that Western country relative to the phenomenon cannot remain a constant value which does not exclude the possibility of a substantial change of the response of international community to the "brain drain" problem in the future.

Western countries, especially European ones, are aware of both positive and negative effects of "brain drain" from their own experience. They also apprehend the detrimental implications of this process for ex-socialist countries. With the account of political and socio-economic transformations ongoing in the post-socialist world, the West is objectively interested in dumping of such consequences. For this reason, one cannot doubt now that in resolving the problem of "brain drain" from countries of CEE, CIS and Russia it is their ally. In any case, at the present time the negative effects of this problem are more sensitive for both East and West than the positive ones which still can be regarded as merely potential advantages.

"Brain drain" has clearly divided the world community into two groups. One of them represents countries which are mere donors of intellectual elite (former socialist states), while another - countries which are mainly recipients of scientific and technological personnel from donor states (developed countries of the West and newly industrialized countries). The first of these groups experiences mainly detrimental effects of the process of intellectual emigration, whereas the second is bound to bear a heavy economic burden of acceptance and absorption of the emigrant flow. Furthermore, the process of "brain drain" which is now beyond any international control substantially increases the probability of a chaotic proliferation of nuclear technologies, chemical, biological and other dangerous weapons over numerous countries as a result of non-controllable emigration of scientists and engineers from the former USSR to various places of the world.

Neither East nor West are interested in such course of developments which at the present time makes their positions substantially closer in respect of this problem. Moreover, both sides are deeply interested in success of market transformations in the former socialist camp for which "brain drain" creates great obstacles, restricts the possibilities of their access to the world market engendering additional sources of social tension and counteraction in respect of the reform ongoing in these countries.

Under such conditions potential advantages resulting from the inflow of an additional intellectual elite come to the second front for the West, whereas the problems of restriction of "brain drain "from the CEE, CIS and Russia and preservation of their R&D potentials obtain top priority. In certain sense such support becomes even more essential than national efforts of former socialist countries in maintaining their scientific and technological potential.

At the present time there is no sufficiently reliable "brain drain" statistics either in the East, or West, or in international organizations. For this reason, a profound study of the problem is a matter of a distant future. Nevertheless, this problem has already become a focus of attention of public and official bodies of the West. Their response makes it possible to come to a conclusion that nearly all Western states have already taken or are taking steps for rendering assistance to science of the former socialist countries in order to prevent a non-controllable "brain drain" from them. And though this assistance still is of a non-coordinated character, not always efficient and has its negative symptoms requiring a special investigation, nevertheless it is being already effected and gaining scale and momentum.

On the part of Western countries the most active participant of this process is FEDERAL REPUBLIC of GERMANY that treats this problem within the framework and subject to the "General concept of the government of FRG relative to the progress of democracy and social market economy in countries of Central and Eastern Europe and the CIS".

Germany renders assistance to the R&D potentials of ex-socialist countries in a number of areas:

1. Federal Ministry of Education and Sciences, in particular,

- supports structural changes and renovation of the system of higher education, courses of education by correspondence, financial aid to updating scientific libraries, etc. In total, in 1993 for this purposes the Ministry allocated 7.3 mln. DM.;
- elaborates recommendations on legal aspects of restructuring of higher education system subject to the international project "Legal Reform" within the framework of the Council of Europe (FRG allocates for these purposes 0.77 mln. DM up to the year 1995);
- provides finances for exchange of experience in modernization of the system of higher education (1992 - 254,000 DM, 1993-1994 - 520,000 DM, 1995 - 130,000 DM);
- allocates money to the German Research Association for organization of programs of assistance to science in countries of CEE and the former USSR; support of scientific events in these countries and abroad, in particular, funding of participation of scholars from the West in conferences and other scientific forums held in Germany, covering expenses connected with the stay of Eastern scientists and engineers in German research and educational institutions for a period of up to 6 months as well as transport and other expenses (in 1993 2.5 mln. DM were allocated for these purposes);
- creates centres of cooperation in higher education (in 1992 the Federal Ministry of Education and Science allocated for the development of such centers in Tubingen 142,000 DM and in Kassel - 128,000 DM); the cooperation projects elaborated there cover various

areas of economics, social sciences, law (Tubingen) in which educational institutions from Russia, Poland, Hungary, Baltic states participate.

2. Alexander Gumboldt Foundation

It is engaged in reception of scientific personnel. In 1991 it received 688 scientists, including: 2 - from Estonia, 55 - from Bulgaria, 45 - from the former Yugoslavia, 5 - from Latvia, 12 - from Lithuania, 152 - from Poland, 67 - from Romania, 190 - from the former USSR, 97 - from the former Czechoslovakia, 63 - from Hungary.

3. Programme of the German Service of Academic Exchanges

In 1991 2,796 scholars were received within the framework of the programme "Exchange of scientists in partnership with East-European countries". Under the programme "Research visits/new invitations" 200 persons visited Germany in 1991, 537 persons got financial support under the programme "Participation of university professors and researchers from Eastern, Central and South-Eastern Europe in conferences in Germany".

4. Non-University Research Institutions and Foundations

(a) Max Planck Society

In 1991 the Max Planck Society elaborated a pilot programme stimulating cooperation with the former socialist countries using funds raised by the German industry (1 mln. DM). Cooperation projects jointly elaborated by Max Planck Institute and its counterparts from CEE countries initially covered a period of 2-3 years since 1991 regarding it as a term for strengthening positions of the partners. Actual expenses in 1991 were 1.3 mln. DM, the deficit was compensated by the Society itself. In addition, Max Planck Society allocated 1.3 mln. DM for 1992 for a financial support of scientists from ex-socialist countries.

In 1992 the Federal Ministry of Research and technologies allocated to Max Planck Society 0.8 mln. DM under the programme "Special visits of researchers from CEE and countries of the former USSR". More than 0.3 DM was used for financing cooperation with research institutions of Russia; the remaining sum was distributed as assistance to R&D centers in the Ukraine, Latvia, Bulgaria, former Czechoslovakia, Poland, Romania, Hungary.

(b) **Volkswagen Foundation**

This organization granted 7.5 mln. DM for implementation of the "Academic programme with CEE partners - stipends to young scientists". The objective of the Foundation - to render assistance to young scholars majoring in humanitarian and social sciences.

The organization responsible for implementation of this programme is Confederation of German Academies of Sciences in Meintz. [1].

United Kingdom

The United Kingdom shows a positive attitude to international exchanges of scientists and specialists, following, however, the interests of national security.

The British government does not tend to control these exchanges considering it a matter of the people and institutions concerned. Nevertheless, it supports such initiatives and takes part in implementation of individual projects.

A number of scientific exchange projects with the former USSR and countries of CEE has been implemented by the Royal Society. At the present time it carries out programmes of training specialists with academic degrees from Hungary, Czechia, Poland which are supported jointly by both state and private foundations. In 1993 a new programme of cooperation with Bulgaria was also launched. After 1987/1988 the number of exchanges with countries of CEE (without the former GDR) organized by the Royal Society increased from 100 to 200 and expenses grew from 60,000 to 450,000 pounds sterl.

The Royal Society signed agreements on cooperation with the RAS and with academies of sciences of some new independent states (Ukraine, Georgia, Lithuania, Latvia, Estonia) envisaging most diverse forms of assistance to international contacts between scientists of Russia and the above-mentioned countries.

The government of Great Britain allocated for 1992/1993 670,000 p.st. for financial support of Russian scientists (subscriptions for scientific literature, short-term missions abroad, funding of participation in international conferences, etc.). Joint research is especially encouraged.

At the beginning of the 80's the ORSAS programme was established for granting stipends to foreign students. Under this programme the stipends are also given to post-graduate students from the former USSR and East-European states: their number increased from 22 in 1990 to 64 in 1991. [2].

Recently the government of Great Britain formed a "Know-How Foundation" which was intended to provide consulting services and transfer of knowledge to republics of the former USSR and East-European states to support democratic transformations in them. This foundation is used mainly for backing projects in the sphere of finances and management, and certain scientific-and-technological projects as well. For example, modernization of tractor-manufacturing plant "Ursus" and development of food industry in Poland, establishment of an open educational center in Budapest (Hungary), organization of a communication center for ecological monitoring in Czechia and others.

Great Britain cooperates with European Union in arranging research and engineering exchanges with East-European countries (programmes PHARE and TACIS of EU technical assistance to ex-socialist states. Besides, it also takes part in the workshop of the European commission on realization of the idea of establishment of an International Association of Assistance to Cooperation with Scientists of CIS Countries on the basis of Belgian legislation.

AUSTRIA

Austria pursues its policy in respect of intellectual emigration from post-socialist states on the basis of two principles. On the one hand, it considers that a broad propagation of R&D results contributes to a growth of living conditions in all countries associated with mobility of scientists and specialists. On the other hand, it finds that their mobility between East and West brings benefits to recipient countries only, while emigrants' home countries suffer political, economic and intellectual damages.

That is why, Austria comes out for controlling the "brain drain" process by way of allocation of financial resources to countries of CEE and the former Soviet Union for weakening the motives for emigration and for increasing attractiveness of a research work at home. In particular, Austrian government offers a growing number of scholarships to citizens of CEE and CIS countries, simultaneously taking measures preventing their stay in Austria for permanent residence. Widely practiced is students' exchanges and establishment of various programmes for education of foreign students in Austria. The Federal Ministry of Science and Higher Education allocated $8 mln. for these purposes in 1990, $13 mln. - in 1991. In 1992/1993 academic year Austria received over 3,500 researchers, professors and students from CEE countries. [3].

Austria takes an active part in multilateral programmes of exchanges of students, professors, researchers, and scientific information. It pays a substantial contribution to TEMPUS programmes in which two countries of European Union and partners from CEE countries also participate. In 1993 Austria offered a new multilateral "Programme of exchange in research between universities of Central Europe" (CEEPUS) with participation of CEE countries, Austria and Italy. This is an open programme which may be joined by other West-European countries. It has a built-in mechanism of counteraction to "brain drain" due to promotion of scientific exchanges between CEE countries themselves.

Austria put forward the initiative of establishing an International Institute of Mathematical Physics named after Erwin Schroedinger which is financed mainly by Austrian government. In the future the Institute will become a permanent organization for a joint research work of specialists in this specific area from both East and West countries.

ITALY

Italian government carries out a whole system of measures intended for training and research work of scientists and specialists from countries of CEE and the former Soviet Union. It tends to make sure that such measures would guarantee a maximum possible positive effect of mutual exchanges, while preventing an excessive and undesirable "brain drain" from these countries.

The major part of international relations of this kind is supervised by the National Research Council coordinating its activity with the Ministry of Foreign Affairs and Ministry of Higher Education, Science and Technological Research. The priority areas of the Council's activity are interrelated with appropriate national R&D development programmes and obligations of Italy in international research programmes and projects.

In 1990 the Council allocated 46 bln.lire (about $40 mln.) for such international cooperation which were distributed in the following way:

1. Department of international relations (in 1992 the budget of this department was about 10 bln. lire):
   (a) bilateral agreements between the Council and respective foreign organizations;
   (b) major international projects;
   (c) subscriptions for literature for international research organizations;
   (d) financial support of foreign participants of international seminars, congresses and other events organized by the Council in Italy, as well as bilateral seminars with participation of representatives of academic institutions of Italy and foreign countries.

2. National research committees (in 1990 such committees invested 5 bln.lire in elaboration of bilateral research projects; in addition, for implementation of a number of multilateral research projects such as EUREKA more than 10 bln. lire were allocated and additional 2 bln. lire were spent for other areas of international cooperation.

3. Invitation of foreign professors (1990 for these purposes, as well as for sending Italian professors abroad about 5.5 bln. lire were spent).

4. Other kinds of cooperation (22 bln.lire).

The institutes taking part in international programmes of the National Council grant a certain number of scholarships for invitation of foreign scientists. For example, in 1992 11 such scholarships were given: 2 - to Hungary, 2 - to Russia, and one for each to Bulgaria, Poland, Ukraine and Lithuania under the programmes of research in chemistry and mathematics. [4].

Bilateral accords on scientific-and-technological cooperation are signed on the basis of intergovernmental agreements on collaboration in science and culture.

The cooperation between the National Council and its foreign counterparts (national research organizations and R&D offices and agencies) is effected by way of exchanges between scholars for elaboration and implementation of joint research programmes of interest for both sides or of a special priority for one of them, as well as by organization of seminars, conferences and other scientific events, joint publications, exchanges of R&D results. The partner country usually pays transport expenses, while the host country bears all costs of stay in Italy.

At the present time Italy has 34 bilateral agreements with the majority of European countries, certain states of Latin America, countries of the former Soviet union, China and Japan.

About 1,000 exchanges occur every year and the major part of them relates to CEE countries. The reason is in that quotas for these countries are about 400 men-months a year, whereas for West-European countries - 250 men-months. This predomination, in turn, is explained by the fact that CEE countries preferred organization of exchanges on an equivalent basis, whereas research institutions of Western Europe and Latin America used other forms.

As regards scientific disciplines, the overwhelming majority of agreements with CEE countries relate to physics, chemistry, mechanical engineering, social sciences. The major part of the agreements has been signed with Russian, Polish and Hungarian Academies of Sciences.

The National Council of Italy and the RAS have an extensive exchange of probationers and scholars on the project on physics of neutrons jointly elaborated and implemented by Institute of Nuclear Physics of the RAS and Monte Bianco Institute and Institute of Cosmogeophysics in Turin.

Cooperation in Higher Education

The scale of this area of cooperation can be illustrated by the fact that in 1991 the Ministry of Higher Education and Science of Italy had more than 1,000 international agreements with the following geographical distribution: European Union - 36%, USA and Canada - 15%, CEE countries - 13%, Latin America - 12%.

During 1989-1991 Italian universities and universities of East-European countries signed about 180 agreements on cooperation among which the major part relates to natural sciences, humanitarian and social sciences. Universities are independent in determination of the forms and contents of contracts and exchanges with foreign partners, thus bringing flexibility in the character of their international cooperation.

Cooperation of Italy with Ex-Socialist Countries under Programmes of European Union

Out of 318 projects selected for implementation Italy participates in 85, and in 14 of them it takes the role of coordinator, and in 20 - chief executive. In 32 European projects Italy cooperates with Hungary and in 12 - with Poland (two of them are headed by Italy).

Subject to European Programme TEMPUS aiming at cooperation between universities Italy received in 1991/1992 250 professors and lecturers from Bulgaria, Poland, Romania and Yugoslavia. The number of Italian professors visited these countries for the same period was 125 persons.

A special role in maintaining mobility and exchanges is played by "ESAGONAL" initiative which includes 6 countries: Italy, Austria, former Yugoslavia, Hungary, Czechoslovakia and Poland. A direct management of this initiative is effected by the Ministry of Foreign Affairs of Italy. This programme aims at assistance to international cooperation with CEE countries, extension of exchanges of scientists and specialists, provision of a greater number of stipends to foreign students, professors and lecturers.

One of the biggest Italian industrial associations IRI supports special cooperation programs within the framework of European Central Initiative and the Group on Science and Technology elaborated for CEE countries. These programmes stipulate creation and practical use of joint structures for carrying R&D and for mutual transfer of technology between partner countries. Common interests cover such areas as information systems, environment protection, space research.

Consortium "Chitta" maintains cooperation in 10 different areas including organization of R&D, training scientific and engineering personnel, realization of special post-graduate programmes in a close collaboration with universities, research centers and individual industrial companies. Such comprehensive projects help to enlarge the number of fruitful contacts with research and educational institutions, as well as industrial enterprises of CEE countries thus making it possible to soften the acuity of "brain drain" problem in them.

NETHERLANDS

In cooperation with countries of CEE and CIS, the Ministry of Education and Science of the Netherlands during the coming period is going to give preference to Hungary and Russia.

A corresponding memorandum with Hungary was signed in November 1992, a similar agreement on cooperation with the Russian Federation in the R&D sphere was signed in the beginning of 1993. For financing of cooperation with Hungary the Ministry of Education and Science allocated 3.13 mln. guilders up to the year 1995, while for cooperation with Russia for the period 1992-1994 it was intended to allocate 15 mln. guilders (5 mln. guilders a year).

In 1992 subject to the programme of support of Russian science, the Dutch organization of scientific research granted first portion of the total allocated money (see Table 1). It was also expected that about 250 Russian scientists would visit Netherlands every year for training and research. On the other hand, about 100 Dutch scholars would visit Russia every year. Besides, in 1992 the Dutch organization of scientific research made a decision to allocate 3 mln. guilders for a one-time support of researchers and research organizations in the former USSR as anticipation of a more sizeable assistance. The programme of support aims at survival of research teams in Russia and in so doing the priority is given to R&D collectives already co-operating with Dutch scientists and engineers. [5].

Table 1. Expenditures for cooperation with Russia in 1992

Field of science	Number of projects	Financing, guilders
Humanitarian studies	6	1,253,430
Social sciences	13	1,528,700
Exact sciences	30	3,221,400
Biology, oceanology, geophysics	11	1,309,000
Medicine	11	946,970
Engineering sciences	8	614,250

Source: National organization of scientific research.

The Dutch Ministry of Education and Science pays a attention to implementation of programmes of student exchanges with the Ukraine (60,000 guilders), Estonia, Latvia, Lithuania, Georgia, Byelorussia (20,000 guilders to each).

In 1988/89 the Ministry of Education and Science took part in implementation of the Programme of internationalization of the national system of higher education (STIP). Since 1990 annual expenditures for the programme were 10 mln. guilders. Though no special quota is provided for CEE countries in the STIP framework, its funds, nevertheless, are used to support exchanges of scholars from these countries (see Table 2).

Table 2. Number of visits under STIP Programme

Agreement with	CEE country - Netherlands			Netherlands - CEE country		
	1990	1991	1992	1990	1991	1992
Hungary	6	3	8	8	28	
Poland	10	9	12	8	8	6
Russia	-	2	6	-	8	10
Czechoslovakia	7	13	12	1	6	2

Source: Royal Dutch Academy of Arts and Sciences, 1993.

In 1991 the government of Netherlands initiated a programme "Eastern Europe" which is implemented both on bilateral and multilateral basis in the ratio of 50%:50%. The bilateral cooperation is coordinated by the State Secretary on Economy. This part of the programme involves projects of assistance to CEE countries on a bilateral basis with the view to providing infrastructure necessary for carrying out economic reforms. 11 Dutch ministries participate in implementation of the programme. In 1992 65 mln. guilders were allocated for it, in 1993 - a slightly greater amount of money.

Within the framework of cooperation programme "Eastern Europe" the government of Netherlands allocated 10 mln. guilders up to January 1, 1997 with the view to exchanging experience of management with CEE countries. Subject to this programme, about 300 managers from CEE countries will be invited to Netherlands for training and practice for a period of from one week to one year. These managers are selected in CEE countries from governmental organizations, industry, agriculture, health, transport, energy and ecology sectors, etc.

The data on exchanges within the framework of the Dutch organization of scientific research, Foundation of basic research of materials and Technological foundation are shown in Table 3.

Table 3. Exchange between Netherlands and CEE countries

Country	1991		1992	
	Nether.-CEE	CEE-Nether.	Nether.-CEE	CEE-Nether.
Bulgaria	4	3	1	1
C I S	49	59	63	83
Hungary	14	45	17	45
Poland	22	28	10	20
Romania	-	6	-	8
ex-Czecholslovakia	6	19	20	34

Source: Royal Dutch Academy, op.cit.

Netherlands also cooperate with CEE countries on a multilateral basis. In 1993 they took part in implementation of 190 projects of EU cooperation in science and technology with CEE countries out of which 174 projects were aimed at supporting scientists and specialists from Bulgaria, Romania, Czechia, Slovakia, Estonia, Latvia, Lithuania, Hungary and Poland going West for a mission of from 3 to 6 months.

The Dutch government also allocated 575,000 guilders for financing a multilateral research Center for Hungarian and Western scientists in Budapest (Collegium Budapest). The main task of the Center is to prevent "brain drain" from CEE countries. Scholars stay at the Collegium Budapest for 10 months. At the end of 1992 the first group of 20 specialists (10 from CEE countries) started their work at the Collegium.

NORWAY

The government of Norway initiated a long-term programme of cooperation with countries of CEE for a period of 1992-1996. The programme is focused on countries - closest neighbours of Norway - North-Western part of Russia, Baltic states of the former USSR and Poland. One of the top priority areas of cooperation under the programme is education and scientific research.

Prior to this new initiative of Norway a whole number of other programmes existed according to which exchanges of scientists and specialists were effected between Norway and CEE countries as it is illustrated by the data of Table 4. [6].

Table 4.
Citizens of CEE countries visited Norway under
various exchange programmes

Country	East-European programme 1991-1992	North-Baltic programme 1991-1992	Cultural agreements 1989-1992		Total
			State stipends	Special exchanges	
Albania	3				3
Bulgaria	10		17	14	41
Estonia	22	27			49
Yugoslavia	5		18	21	44
Latvia	13	26			39
Lithuania	14	35			49
Poland	19		67	26	112
Romania	8		4	4	16
Russia	7		7	3	17
Czechoslovak	16		58	30	104
Hungary	12		22	21	55

FINLAND

Since 1991 exchanges between scientists and specialists of Finland and those of CEE countries are regulated by Finnish center of international mobility, Academy of Finland, higher educational and research institutions. Statistical data on bilateral exchanges of scientists of Finnish Academy of Sciences with academic institutions of some CEE countries is shown in Table 5.

Table 5.
Bilateral exchanges of scientists of the Academy of Sciences
of Finland with academies of sciences of some CEE countries (1992)

Country	Quota	Finnish scientists		Foreign scientists	
		Persons	Days	Persons	Days
Bulgaria	270	4	61	9	171
Poland	1,050	32	248	75	1,041
Romania	90	4	65	7	105
Czechoslovakia	480	9	76	26	419
Russia	2,520	34	349	71	1,206
Estonia*	90	9	80	13	90

* Since 1992 the Academy of Sciences of Finland has a new
partner - the Scientific Council of Estonia and the new quota of exchanges of scientists and specialists is 1,200 days before the end of
1994. [7]. At the present time protocols of intentions were signed
with Lithuania and Latvia on future cooperation in R&D with the
view to preventing undesirable "brain drain" from these countries.

The data on exchanges of scientists and specialists under programmes of cooperation effected via channels of the Center of international mobility in 1992 are shown in Table 6.

Table 6.
Exchanges of scientists and engineers of the Finnish
Center of International Mobility in 1992

Country	Finnish scientists		Foreign scientists	
	Persons	Days	Persons	Days
Bulgaria	6	465	11	808
Czecholsovakia	19	1,080	27	1,690
Estonia	-	-	2	210
Hungary	37	1,920	25	1,800
Poland	15	1,170	21	2,060
Romania	2	22	3	30

Academy of Sciences of Finland has signed a new agreement
with the Hungarian Academy of Sciences under which several Hungarian professors work a part of an academic year in Finland and
get a salary of a Finnish professor, and the remaining part of the

year is spent in Hungary. This agreement aims at hindering "brain drain" from Hungary.

A new phenomenon in the Finnish Academy of Sciences is applications filed with the Finnish Council on Scientific Research by Finnish scholars who want to invite foreign scientists, mainly from Estonia and Russia, to visit Finland or to take part in joint Finnish-Russian projects. The visiting scientists obtain a grant or a salary as a participant of the R&D project. For example, Finnish Academy supports financially the work of a Russian mathematician, Academician Fadeev, at the University of Helsinki during a part of an academic year. The remaining part of the year is spent by Academician at Sanct-Petersburg where he heads a research team of Russian scientists.

The Council for Scientific Research also provides grants for post-graduate students from CEE countries coming to Finland for preparation of their doctorate thesises.

Together with other Nordic countries Finland takes part in North-Baltic cooperation financially supported by the Nordic Council of Ministers and Nordic Organization for cooperation of research organizations.

FRANCE

This country adheres to a comprehensive approach to solution of the "brain drain" problem in CEE countries. On the one hand, a more severe provisions are introduced into the immigration laws in order to prevent an illegal immigration of foreign intellectuals into the country. On the other hand, measures are taken to retain specialists from CEE countries at home by way of creation appropriate conditions for that at the account of French financing sources.

In doing so, a so-called "bipolar cooperation" method is practiced by way of creation of research pairs or cooperation couples. For example, in the area of mathematics and physics a successful cooperation is effected between Jusse Paris University and Steklov Saint-Petersburg mathematical institute, in molecular biology - between Paster Strassburg Institute and Microbiological Institute in Puschino, Russia.

Certain French companies prefer to involve Russian partners into joint projects directly at their home institutions. For example, an aviation company "Societe Europeen de Propultion" producing engines for "Arian" space rocket already signed 33 contracts with research laboratories of Russia and Ukraine. Signing of 5 more contracts is expected which will provide an opportunity of providing jobs for scientists and specialists of these countries, especially of their military-and-industrial complex, who are facing the threat of unemployment as a result of an improperly thought-out conversion of the defense sector of their economies.

The French National Centre of Scientific Research opened its permanent representation office in Moscow with the view to employing Russian scientists and engineers and preventing them from undesirable emigration from the country, as well as for coordination of bilateral cooperation directly in Russia.

One of the most important areas of solution of the "brain drain" problem in CEE and CIS countries by France is the creation of favourable conditions for scientific and engineering personnel from these countries who go to France for work on a contractual basis, for their successful integration into local scientific communities. For attraction of specialists to France for a contract work specialized companies are formed which proved their efficiency in recruiting the required personnel. For example, 30% of professors and lecturers who got their job at French universities in 1992 were invited from Russian educational institutions.

The main accent is placed on young people who, as a rule, have a better command of the French language, are more dynamic and aggressive, better adaptable to new work and homelife environment, less sensitive to socio-economic conditions of their living. In 1992 the French government provided about 100 stipends for young scientists from the CIS countries of 1 month to 1 year academic term in France. The French Ministry of Industry provides annually about 20 stipends for young scholars from the CIS at the most advanced laboratories of their enterprises both in France and in third countries.

One of promising ways for solving the problem of "brain drain" from CEE countries is education of students from these countries in France at the expenses of its stipend fund. In particular, the French government financed a number of programmes under which students, post-graduates and young specialists from the countries of the former Soviet Union are studying and trained in France.

From January 1, 1991 to April 1, 1992 928 persons came for education purposes to France, including 248 women. The main part of stipends is allocated to exact sciences 400. Out of them 211 are granted to students majoring in physics, 105 - in chemistry, the remaining - mathematics, biology, engineering sciences. A substantial number of stipends is given to those majoring in marketing, commerce, administrative management (214), 130 scholarships are intended for students studying humanities. Students come, most frequently, for one month or two-three weeks (up to 20%). About 10% of students from CEE and CIS countries study in France for 3, 6 and 9 months, 8% - for one year. [8].

JAPAN

In Japan the problem of "brain drain" from the countries of the former Soviet Union and Central and Eastern Europe is regarded in a broader context of political and economic stability, maintaining peaceful political environment and promoting economic development in the Asian-Pacific region.

The main role in scientific and technological cooperation of Japan with foreign countries is played by the Japanese Society for the Promotion of Science (JSPS) which is a semi-governmental organization under the Ministry of Education, Science and Culture. It maintains international scientific contacts with more than 60 countries of the world. In 1992 out of the total budget of the JSPS ($68.7 mln.) 44% were allocated to implementation of international cooperation programs. These programs include, in particular:

1. Scholarships for Foreign Scientists

This programme enables Japanese scholars to invite their foreign colleagues for participation in joint research and in other kinds of scientific activity. Application for granting such scholarships are filed by Japanese scientists desiring to invite their foreign partners to Japan with the JSPS.

2. Post-Doctorate Training Courses

Under this programme scholarships are granted to promising foreign scholars already having a doctor's academic degree. In 1992 they were granted to scientists from 28 countries: countries of OECD, CEE, China and Korea. The candidates for such scholarships are chosen by competent national agencies of individual countries.

3. Bilateral Programmes

The JSPS has bilateral agreements with 45 research institutes in 30 countries of the world, including CEE countries, on exchanges of scientists and specialists, on joint research programmes and projects, on carrying out joint scientific seminars and other scientific events.

4. Programmes of cooperation with South-East Asian countries.

The data illustrating the number of scientists and specialists involved in exchanges of Japan with CEE countries in 1989-1991 are shown in Table 7.

Table 7.
Number of foreign scientists invited to Japan and
Japanese scientists working abroad in 1989-1991

Country	Invited to Japan			Invited from Japan		
	1989	1990	1991	1989	1990	1991
Albania	1	0	0	0	0	0
Bulgaria	12	11	5	3	3	2
Czechoslovakia	9	11	9	1	1	0
Hungary	11	17	19	12	8	4
Poland	19	21	28	5	6	7
Romania	0	0	2	2	0	0
CIS	37	47	51	18	22	26
Yugoslavia	4	3	0	0	0	0
former GDR	5	3	0	0	1	0
Estonia	0	0	2	0	0	0
Latvia	0	0	1	0	0	0

Source: M.Tokaishi. Programmes of Scientific Exchanges between Japan and CEE Countries. OECD Vienna Conference "East-West Mobility of Scientists and Engineers", February 18-19, 1993., p.3.

Japan considers that to prevent "brain drain" from countries of CEE and CIS, an adequate financial and technical assistance should be rendered to them for preservation of their R&D potentials. Recently the JSPS initiated a new programme of scientific cooperation with the states newly formed after breakup of the former Soviet Union. The programme is financed at the account of contributions made by industrial enterprises on the initiative of a group of prominent Japanese scientists and engineers.

The programme is governed by a Council consisting of 9 well-known scientists. It has four areas of its activity in support of scientists of the former USSR: (1) joint research projects; (2) assistance to scientists from Russia and other CIS countries invited to Japan for research and training; (3) allocation of grants; (4) other kinds of cooperation. The programme is scheduled for 3 years (1993-1995) and its budget is 100 mln.yen. [9].

A legal basis for Russian-Japanese scientific cooperation is the agreement between governments of Japan and Soviet Union of 1986 (which succeeded the agreement of 1972). The counterparts of the JSPS in the Soviet Union were the Ministry of Higher and Secondary Education and the USSR Academy of Sciences. Since 1992, the Russian side is represented by the Committee of Higher Education (now Ministry) and the Russian Academy of Sciences. According to the JSSS initiative, the expenses associated with missions of Russian scientists and specialists to Japan are borne by the Japanese side.

The JSPS holds that in addition to the Russian Federation, relations in the R&D sphere should be restored with other countries of the former Soviet Union and respective agreements should be signed with each of them on a bilateral basis.

Some legal and organizational measures should be taken in order to make cooperation with CEE countries more efficient, in particular in the sphere of exchanges of scientists and specialists in order to prevent excessive "brain drain" from them.

USA

The United States of America is a traditional center of attraction of people from the whole world seeking freedom, highly paid jobs, opportunities for self-realization, good education for themselves and their children, well-being for their families, feeling of security and happiness.

In 1992 immigration to the USA reached such a scale that was observed only once during the recent 70 years. Only in 1978 its level was higher as a result of a huge inflow of immigrants from countries of Indochina and Cuba. As compared to 1991, the number of immigrants increased by 15.1% and amounted to 810,635 persons. The major part of immigrants were from Mexico (91,332 persons), Vietnam (77,727), Philippines (59,179) former republics of the USSR (43,590), Dominican Republic (40,840). It is expected that by the end of the 90's 800,000 to 900,000 persons will immigrate in the USA annually. [10].

At the present time US immigration policy is based on the new Immigration Law passed on November 29, 1990 declaring such principles of admittance to the country as reunification of families, other humanitarian considerations (violation of ethnic, religious and human rights and freedoms in home countries, etc.), as well as need in representatives of professions for which a high demand is noted in the USA. Now the federal government controls immigration into the country by means of quotas for different countries and categories of persons. One of the main goals of the Law is to increase an inflow of high-skill personnel and, not in the last place, from countries of CEE and the former Soviet Union.

For those professions where a deficit of labour force is especially acute, immigration becomes a main source of solution of the problem: the quota based on professional criteria is enlarged from 54,000 to 140,000 persons a year. There is another provision in the Law which provides issuance of 10,000 immigration visas to foreigners who want to invest at least $1 mln. in one of US cities (on their option) or $500,000 in rural areas, or in the regions most suffered from unemployment. [11].

Immigration is not a threat for the USA, because this is a country of immigrants since the moment of its foundation. The USA are interested in a continuous infusion of a fresh intellectual labour force, because the same trends are observed in America as elsewhere in the developed world: aging of the population and decline of birth rates. Nevertheless, this does not exclude origination of certain social tension in this or that sphere of the American economy associated with the expenditures (federal, local, municipal) for municipal housing, creation of new jobs, social needs, etc. in favour of immigrants. That is why mass inflows of immigrants cause a noticeable opposing response in the country both on the official and popular levels.

For example, a considerable inflow of programmers from Russia to the USA during recent years who agree to smaller payment rates resulted in a professional dumping in the country, thus reducing wages and salaries of the domestic specialists of this profession. The latter now insist on endorsement of a law subject to which the companies using immigrant labour force should pay additional taxes. On the contrary, managers of the firms employing foreign (in particular Russian) specialists hold that their labour makes it possible to considerably reduce production costs in creation of software in America and thus improve its position in the world market of this intellectual product. In this manner the interests of managers of some American companies collide with those of "native" scientists and engineers, high-skill workers. This collision finds its reflection in a bill which is now under consideration in the US Congress that stipulates restriction of annual immigration quotas to the USA to the number of 300,000 persons.

Today the situation is developing in favour of American entrepreneurs, but the cost of foreign intellectual manpower is steadily growing and domestic US specialists become more fully aware that they are facing a serious problem pregnant with a possible social tension and that a reasonable way out should be found by pursuing a more flexible immigration policy.

In a broader context of cooperation with countries of CEE and the former Soviet Union in resolving their "brain drain" problem this means finding funds, new forms and methods of keeping the R&D personnel of these countries at home, providing them with new jobs and adequate salaries enabling their decent life in their own countries.

For example, with the view to minimize unemployment in the Russian space industry and thus prevent Russian space technology specialists from emigration abroad a special agreement was reached between the USA and Russia during Russian Premier V.Chernomyrdin's visit to Washington in June 1994 about cooperation in a project ($400 mln. worth) of development of a space station.

As part of the United States' effort to work with the Commonwealth of Independent States - CIS - (or Newly Independent States - NIS - in American terminology) as they make the transition to democracy and a freemarket economy, the US Agency for International Development (USAID) established a Task Force in April 1992. To coordinate and implement the assistance programmes, USAID provided $235 mln. in its own FY (fiscal year) 1992 funds. An additional $147 mln. for CIS projects were authorized by the US Congress for FY 1993 under the Freedom Support Act. [12].

To support this effort, USAID missions are now open in Moscow (Russia), Kiev (Ukraine), Yerevan (Armenia) and Almaty

(Kazakhstan). The Moscow mission serves Russia; Kiev serves Ukraine, Belarus and Moldova; Yerevan serves the Caucasus region; and Almaty serves the Central Asian republics.

As of April 1993, USAID has authorized and begun implementing ten projects in the CIS. They are:

Project 0001: Special Initiatives
Project 0002: Energy Efficiency and Market Reform
Project 0003: Environmental Policy and Technology
Project 0004: Health Care Improvement
Project 0005: Private Sector Initiatives
Project 0006: Food Systems Restructuring
Project 0007: Democratic Pluralism Initiatives
Project 0008: Housing Sector Reform
Project 0009: Economic Restructuring and Financial Reform
Project 0012: CIS Exchanges and Training

In addition, two projects were in the authorization process in April 1993:

Project 0010: Foundation for Technical Assistance (Eurasia
           Foundation)
Project 0011: Enterprise Funds

The NIS Task Force also has an Office of Emergency Humanitarian Assistance which is engaged in coordinating a number of ongoing emergency food and medical programs in the CIS.

The projects help the CIS countries to cope with the "brain drain" problem through creation of new jobs and keeping local specialists at home, as well as by providing them with the opportunity of obtaining knowledge and expertise in the United States. Thus, within the framework of Project 0001 a Special American Business Internship Training (SABIT) has placed approximately 250 scientists and executives from CIS countries in 150 different US firms for 3- to 6- months internships to provide first-hand knowledge of and experience working in a market economy. Under Project 0002 in summer 1992 a delegation of senior energy officials and managers from Kazakhstan and Kyrgyzstan was brought by USAID to the USA to learn about the American energy sector, technology and product. In June 1993 a group of 250 Russian bankers came to the

USA for training in the banking sphere at the University of Fairfield, Connecticut, for eight weeks. [13].

In their efforts to keep personnel of the former Soviet Union countries from emigration the USA also practice "on-site" training projects, i.e. directly at research institutions and production enterprises of specialists' homeland. In so doing, new forms of tripartite cooperation are used with participation of third countries having an extensive experience of relations with certain regions of the ex-USSR and proper understanding of their specific needs and conditions. For example, within the framework of Project 0001 the USA and Turkey will work on a bank training and maternal/child health program in Central Asia. There is also a joint US-Israel cooperative program under which technical assistance and training is provided to senior government officials, farm planners and managers throughout Central Asia.

Another new form of organizational solution of the "brain drain" problem in the CIS with the assistance of the USA is establishment of partnerships or other kinds of joint ventures. For example, through Children's Health System and the American International Health Alliance, 20 partnerships have been established between US hospitals and health care institutions in 9 CIS republics. These provide clinical and administrative training both in the USA and the CIS. Partnerships in all 12 CIS republics were expected by 1994. [14].

Being aware of possible unemployment in Russia as a result of conversion of the defense sector and restructuring of its national economy and regarding it as an impetus for emigration and a mass escape of scientists, engineers and other specialists to commerce, small business, USAID has budgeted more than $121 mln. for FY 1992 and 1993 to support private sector development in the CIS. The program focuses on three strategic area: privatization, trade and investment, and small business development. A new Enterprise Fund was formed under this program which provided $65 mln. to support small and medium enterprises in Russia in 1993. To assist Russia in privatization, the USA intends to invest additional $190 mln. in 1994. In total, in 1995 the USA plans to allocate $450 mln. to support reinforcement of democratic institutes and market reforms in Russia.

To support the development of a market-oriented housing sector in the CIS with the view to improving dwelling conditions for local specialists so as to minimize the role of this factor in emigration moods, USAID has budgeted $16 mln. in FY 1992 and 1993. The goal of this program is to reduce high public subsidies in the housing sector, transfer key functions from the public to the private sector, and develop housing finance mechanisms. Long-term resident advisers and short-term specialists will pursue these goals in partnership with public and private sector officials in the CIS. USAID is also providing, through three US firms specializing in housing and urban management, long-term advisers to provide policy advice, technical assistance and training to local public and private institutions. This is complemented by a network of short-term specialists on mission to Russia, Armenia and Kazakhstan. [15].

In accordance with the FREEDOM Support Act, USAID has budgeted $30 mln. in FY 1993 to provide citizens of the CIS the opportunity to participate in US-sponsored exchanges, training (both short- and long-term) and institutional partnerships supportive of ongoing economic and political transformation processes in the CIS. Project activities will occur in the USA where CIS citizens can receive not only skills training, but also first-hand exposure to US management techniques, institutional arrangements, free market economies and democratic principles. Within this project framework short-term (4-6 weeks) training is targeted at private and public sector CIS leaders and professionals who are in position to effect rapid change at home. Long-term training covers degree and non-degree graduate-level programs currently not available in CIS institutions in areas which support the CIS transition to a market economy. Particular attention is given to the training of trainers. USAID has also provided $16.25 mln. to support administer graduate and undergraduate exchanges, sister university programs, local and regional self-government exchanges, private sector exchanges and Freedom Support grants. [16].

In addition to the above-mentioned and other governmental and semi-governmental bodies, programmes and projects aiming at support of science and technology in countries of CEE and the former Soviet Union and prevention of excessive and undesirable emigration from them, in the USA there are a number of various foundations and funds pursuing the same objectives.

Among them the leading role belongs to the George Soros Foundation which is one of the main founders, together with the Russian Science Fund, of the International Science Foundation (ISF) established in 1993 and intended to support basic research in Russia. The goal of the ISF is to encourage and keep up the best researchers of the former Soviet Union, to provide them the opportunity of continuing their work at home during this very difficult period of development of the national R&D sphere.

The ISF has a capital of $100 mln. which is a charity gift by G.Soros. During 2 years (1993-1994) the Foundation fully distributed this money for supporting basic sciences in the CIS and former Baltic republics of the ex-USSR. The ISF provides grants of short- and long-term assistance under the supervision of the Executive Committee consisting of well-known scholars and headed by Prof. Dr. James D.Watson, Nobel Prize winner, Cold-Spring Harbor, USA. As short-term aid scientists got 26,000 individual grants of $500 each and 1,000 grants of $1,500 for distribution in research teams. Long-term grants (for a period of up to 2 years) of not more than $100,000 and to the total amount of $46 mln. are given to individual scientists and small research collectives on the grounds of their scientific qualifications, as well as the scientific value and substantiation of the proposed project. [17].

In order to facilitate participation of scientists from the former USSR in international scientific conferences and other events, the ISF set a program of grants to cover travel expenses. In 1993 the Foundation financed trips of about 2,000 scholars to 400 scientific conferences outside the former Soviet Union.

With the view to restoring the system of receiving foreign scientific information by Russian libraries that was nearly broken in 1991 due to shortage of funds, the ISF initiated a program of delivery and distribution of the most popular journals on natural sciences.

For the development of information exchange between scientists of the CIS and Baltia and accession to international communication systems the ISF established a special telecommunication program which has four main goals:

(1) assistance in creation of systems of international communication accessible to all communication systems of research and educational institutions;

(2) development of infrastructure of communications and information exchange inside the country;

(3) consultations and assistance in coordination and organization of training technical personnel in operation of communication systems in research and educational institutions;

(4)   extensive training of users of information in research and educational organizations.

The Foundation is also engaged in other spheres of activity, in many cases in cooperation with other charity organizations, mostly foreign, for allocation of funds intended for preservation and development of the R&D potential of Russia and other countries of the former USSR.

The executive and working bodies of the Foundation are in the USA (Washington and New York respectively), but it is the Foundation's policy to perform the major part of work in local representation offices. The majority of employees work at Moscow office, ISF representation missions are also in Kiev (Ukraine), Almaty (Kazakhstan), Bishkek (Kyrgyzstan), Vilnius (Lithuania), Kishinev (Moldova), Minsk (Belorus), Riga (Latvia), Tallinn (Estonia), Tbilisi (Georgia), as well as in Sanct-Petersburg and Novosibirsk (Russia).

Another American foundation ($3 mln.) was established by John and Catherine MacArthur to support young Russian scientists, nuclear arms conversion programs and to preserve Russia's unique but underfunded resources: archives and botanical collections. In addition, the Foundation provides grants for holding US-Russian conferences on social, political and cultural aspects of science and engineering within the framework of the Science, Technology and Society Program sponsored by the Massachusetts Institute of Technology. Five such conferences have already been conducted.

The US National Scientific Foundation (NSF) also takes part in cooperation with scientists in the former Soviet Union. For these purposes it allocated $25 mln. NSF encourages United States participation in international science and engineering activities in accordance with the large stake that the USA has in assisting in the transformation of the science and technology systems and in resolving the "brain drain" problem in countries of Eastern Europe and, in particular, the successor states of the former Soviet Union. In addition to supporting cooperative research between individual investigators, NSF International Programs encourages projects that aim to establish long-term links between US science and technology centers and centers of excellence in the region, on regional as opposed to bilateral projects and on interactions mediated by professional science and engineering societies. A long-term objective is to assist scientists and engineers in the region to become fully functioning members of the international scientific community.

Types of activities supported by NSF International Programs include the following [18]:

1. **Cooperative research** involving a partnership between at least one United States principal investigator/research institution and a foreign counterpart investigator/institution.
2. **Joint seminars and workshops.**
3. **Planning visits.**
4. **Post-Doctoral and Junior Investigator Research Fellowships.**
5. **Dissertation Enhancement Awards.**

International Programs will also consider proposals for other types of activities that help advance NSF's objectives for improving the participation and understanding of the United States science and engineering communities in international efforts to support R&D potentials of countries of CEE and the former Soviet Union and to alleviate the "brain drain" problem facing them.

One of promising areas of cooperation between the USA and the CIS in preservation of national R&D potential with the help of American investments is establishment of international research centers on the basis of already existing leading research institutes of these countries, as well as creation of new, CIS-based international research organizations aimed at providing proper labour and home-life conditions for scientific personnel to keep it from emigration abroad. In so doing, the USA pool their efforts with other Western partners. For example, in February 1992, the United States, Germany and Russia agreed to open an international R&D center near Moscow. Its main aim is to support Russian scientist engaged, primarily, in the nuclear industry. A similar center will be opened in Kiev. The United States, Canada, Ukraine and Sweden signed respective agreements in June 1992. The task of both centers is to help researchers and engineers engaged in programs of development of nuclear, biological and chemical weapons, intercontinental missiles to shift to the manufacture of civil products; they are also intended to assist the defense industry in conversion of military production.

At the end of November 1992 an agreement was signed on establishment of another nuclear research center in Russia. The United States and Western Europe will contribute $25 mln. each, Japan will allocate $20 mln. for this purpose. It is hoped that this center will halt the outflow of Russian nuclear physicists to "hot spots" of the planet.

The United States, Japan, European Union and Russia have also signed an agreement on a joint development of an experimental prototype of a nuclear-fusion reactor. They will share, on equal footing, the project costs of about $1.2 bln. [19].

It should be noted that in rendering assistance to science and technology in countries of the former Soviet Union the USA pay attention to the state of the R&D sphere in various regions of this great country and, in the first place, in Russia. A great interest is shown in support of those regions of Russia where the situation in science becomes rather tense and might result in unemployment of scientists and specialists with related social discontent and growing emigration moods. One of such regions is, of course, Siberia where about 100 research institutions associated in 9 complex scientific centers function under the aegis of the Siberian Division of the Russian Academy of Sciences. Some of these institutions are turned now into international research centers (at the moment there are 14 such organizations), many of them with American participation on a bilateral or multilateral basis.

Another region of interest - Moscow oblast' (region) where world-known research centers (such as Dubna (nuclear physics), Protvino (particle accelerator installations), etc.) are located together with about a hundred of other R&D organizations engaged in different spheres of modern science and technology. Thus, on the basis of the Noginsk physico-chemical research center a zone of joint scientific entrepreneurship is arranged in the form of a so-called Chernogolovka (science city) technopolis. Institutes and administration of Moscow oblast' received many proposals from US universities, in particular from Stanford, California, Washington, for participation in establishment of innovation centers, technoparks, technological green-houses in the region. An agreement was signed between the regional administration and "Boeing" company on organization of a research center which later will develop into a technopolis. In December 1991 an inter-regional general agreement on cooperation (including the R&D sphere) was signed by Moscow region and the state of Indiana (USA) stipulating participation of

American partners in regional scientific and educational projects. The number of such "sister regions" in Russia and USA is growing.

Other forms of support to Russian science and scientists comprise joint research on a commercial basis at Russian research institutions, supplies of modern scientific equipment and instruments, direct contacts between research institutes and scientists, invitation of Russian scientists to work abroad (also in the third countries) on a contractual basis, etc.

On the company level, Sun Microsystems Inc. was the first American firm to extend support to Russian scientists, preventing at least 100 software specialists from emigration. The company employed a group of 50 Russian computer scientists and engineers in 1991 and another such group in 1993. The company offered them work on a contract basis, opened a well-equipped laboratory in Moscow for elaboration and manufacture of new computer systems. [20].

Two other American companies - American Telephone and Telegraph Bell Laboratories (ATTBL) and Corning Glass signed contracts with Russian scientists for research in fiber optics. ATTBL signed a contract with the Institute of General Physics, Russian Academy of Sciences, subject to which 100 scientists out of 1,200 employees of the Institute would be engaged in work for the American company. Corning signed an agreement with 115 researchers and engineers working at the Vavilov Optical Institute in St. Petersburg, the largest world research center in optics, and at the Institute of Silicate Chemistry which is known for its achievements in optical glass technology.

The famous Boeing Corporation and several Russian research institutes have agreed to open a center near Moscow for joint R&D projects in the aircraft industry. Boeing will finance the center and sign contracts with Russian specialists. It plans to jointly develop new methods of modeling flying apparatus, life support systems for orbiting satellites and stations, manufacture of new materials for aerospace industry.

More examples illustrating such US-Russian cooperation can be cited and it is likely that their number will substantially increase after Russian Premier V.Chernomyrdin's visit to the USA in June 1994 when a series of bilateral cooperation agreements in various areas was signed. Among them, in particular, is an agreement on cooperation in space technology for which $400 mln. are allocated for 4 years, including $20 mln. for the development of space research.

Additional money are provided for Moscow Khrunichev Space Design Office engaged in the development of "Energiya" carrier rockets. All these examples show that the assistance to Russia (as well as to other ex-Soviet republics and CEE countries) is considered and practically rendered by the USA in a broader context of combined scientific-and-technological and immigration policies.

By the way, the US immigration policy in respect of granting visas to citizens of Russia, other countries of CIS and CEE is continuously improved towards a more efficient selection of would-be newcomers. Since 1994 a new alternative program for getting immigration visas was initiated by the US government in the form of a lottery in which any citizen of the Russian Federation and other CIS and CEE countries can take part irrespective of availability of close relatives in the USA. The information about candidates for a "green card" in the USA under this lottery program is introduced into a computer which then chooses the winners on an objective and non-prejudiced basis. The total number of visas granted in this manner is 55,000. The quota for Russia is 3,850. [21]. A winner may come to the USA for a temporary work together with his (her) family. It is no doubt that among those 3,850 persons there will be a substantial number of Russian scientists and engineers willing to try their luck in the United States.

The geography of assistance to Russia's science and technology also includes countries of South-East Asia. In South Korea, for example, several Korean-Russian joint laboratories are in operation. Korea offers employment contracts to Russian scientists and engineers. Such matters are handled by government research centers such as Korean Institute for Science and Technology (KIST) and by private corporations (De Woo, Samsung, etc.). The KIST which runs a Korean-Russian center, signed a cooperation agreement with the Russian Academy of Sciences for a period of five years under which 74 joint projects were approved. Korea is interested in Russian basic research, conversion of military production to civilian purposes, new technologies and software. Specialists in these fields are invited to work in Korean research institutions.

During his visit to Russia in May 1994, Mr. Kim Yong Sam, President of the Republic of Korea said: "Russia is a country with a great economic potential based on a well-developed basic research and advanced science-intensive technology, rich natural resources and a high educational level of the population. The development of

relations between the two nations on the basis of mutual complementation of their economies will be accelerated, if we manage to
combine our industrial technology and our experience of operation
in the world market with the Russian potential". [22].

Asian countries prefer to invite the intellectual elite to work on a
contract basis, rather than to encourage its immigration. Local sociologists explain this preference by pointing to a great ethnic and cultural difference, different way of life, traditions, religion, climatic
conditions, etc.

A more flexible approach is demonstrated by countries of Latin
America which combines both immigration and contractual work of
scientists and engineers from countries of CEE and especially of the
former Soviet Union. The respective policies and practice of individual countries of Latin America are described in more detail in the
chapter devoted to analysis of the geographic and professional
structure of emigration from countries of Russia and the CIS.

Nevertheless, it is quite clear that the problem of "brain drain"
from Russia, other CIS states, as well as from countries of CEE
takes now an international character and in its solution nearly all
world community is involved. The response to it of each country
concerned depends on its specific political, social and economic
conditions so that in many cases countries of the world tend to pool
their efforts in coping with this problem, in cooperation with countries of CEE and the former Soviet Union aiming at preservation of
their national R&D potentials and prevention of undesirable "brain
drain", on a bilateral basis, or on a multilateral level within the
framework of international organizations.

3.4. POSITION OF INTERNATIONAL ORGANIZATIONS WITH RESPECT TO "BRAIN DRAIN" FROM CIS AND CEE COUNTRIES

The problem of ethnic and labour migration of the population
during recent years becomes one of the global problems of our time.
Among measures aiming at its solution a special attention is paid
by the world community to regulation of the process of intellectual
emigration ("brain drain") from CEE and CIS countries which now
takes on growing proportions and gains momentum, thus bringing
certain tension into international migration flows.

Western countries do not fence themselves off this process and
on national and international levels they start to study and analyze

it so as to understand its reasons and character, to undertake appropriate measures influencing its nature, scale, geographical and professional structure in order that countries of CEE, of the former Soviet Union and the global community as a whole would bear minimum hardships resulting from this growing wave of emigration.

The international organizations during recent years pay a special attention to the movement of scientific and engineering personnel on the European continent, evaluation of its present state and possible consequences.

It is understood that East-West mobility of scientists and engineers should be regarded in a broader context of a market of labour of intellectual personnel. In a number of countries of CEE and the former Soviet Union the number of scientists and engineers exceeds the available possibilities of their employment dictated by the present economic situation and existing financial resources. As a result, there is a certain excess of scholars and specialists and the level of their salaries is essentially lower than in the West.

In addition to uncertainty and bad conditions for a professional activity, another motif of emigration is a political instability in a number of countries of the region under consideration, lack of a proper status of scientific-and-technological intelligentsia and corresponding absence of adequate conditions of work and homelife usually guaranteed by a civilized society of Western countries.

The situation in the market of intellectual labour force in countries of CEE and CIS is aggravated due to release of manpower resulting from conversion of the defense sector of their economies which causes a growing concern in the West as a factor noticeably affecting the scale, structure and qualitative character of European and other world markets of labour force.

In this connection, a subject of a general anxiety of the West is elaboration of a system of measures restraining "brain drain" and "brain waste" in East-European countries within the framework of a pragmatic approach intended to derive the maximum possible benefit for all the concerned participants of the "brain drain" process which has already taken an irreversible character.

Western approach to assistance to countries of CEE and the former Soviet Union, Russia in particular, was formulated in general by Mr. Augustino Forti, Director of the UNIDO International Center for Science and High Technologies (Triest, Italy) during his visit to Moscow at the end of 1992: "Russia is going through hard times, and Europe came to lend it a helping hand. But no matter how it is important today to send grain, foodstuffs and medicines to Russia, this aid is of a this-minute nature, whereas assisting Russia in research, development of new technologies, and restructuring of its industry is consistent with the long-term interests of both Russia and Europe. For this reason, the West should give top priority to aiding Russian science". [1].

To prevent undesirable and excessive "brain drain" from CEE and CIS countries, the West finds it expedient to intensify East-West cooperation on a bilateral basis, as well as by way of coordinated multilateral efforts in both parts of Europe and between them. In so doing, a considerable portion of the preparation work in this direction should be realized by East-European countries themselves irrespective of the existing economic constraints in order to create conditions necessary and sufficient to maintain their national R&D potentials and their integration into the global scientific community.

This problem has also an essential political aspect and certain ideological nature. What is the role of science and technology in the society in general? What is their place during the period of transition from the command-administrative to a market economy in the socio-economic and culture-civilization progress of post-communist societies? In what manner the scientific and technological factor can catalyze the process of their integration into the global system of political, economic and cultural cooperation?

In the context of answering these and other related questions the responsibility for the maintenance and development of R&D potentials of East-European countries should be taken by both sides - both East and West which supposes intensification of their cooperation in science and innovation and, in particular, in solution of the problem of "brain drain" in the light of a broader and comprehensive problem of a mutually beneficial exchange of scientists and specialists.

The scale and level of development of Western R&D potential, conditions of work and homelife of Western scientist and specialists, recognition of the leading role of creative intelligentsia in the socio-economic progress of Western society - all this defines attractiveness of the West for "brains" from CEE and the former Soviet Union and, on the other hand, imposes a certain responsibility in the context of regulation of the immigration process and rendering respective assistance to the progress of national science and technology in the former socialist countries.

However, East-West cooperation in science and technology should not be limited only to assistance to East-European and CIS states. Countries of this region have a sufficiently big and valuable stock of R&D results and its use on a mutually beneficial basis in the economies of both East and West can be equally productive for both sides and for the global community on the whole. The access to this R&D stock should become one of objectives of Western policy and it can be achieved by way of a proper regulation of the process of migration of scientists and specialists, finding an optimal solution for the "brain drain" problem.

During recent time Western countries (in particular, within the OECD framework) have taken a number of measures for maintaining and, to some extent, even developing the scientific and technological potential of CEE and CIS countries. Thus, they took steps for lowering the cost of access to scientific information and publications of Western scientists, for introducing preferential financing of participation of East-European scientists and specialists in international scientific conferences and other forums. There were elaborated and started to implement numerous programmes of exchanges of scientists and specialists aiming at the maximum possible reduction of "brain drain".

A considerable number of projects is provided for allocation of grants to young scholars and outstanding representatives of scientific elite for a period of from 6 to 18 months with the provision that on expiration of the grant term they would come back home. As a rule, the receiving Western center is an already existing research institution. Nevertheless, a whole number of new research organizations were formed specially for creating proper conditions of research work for East-European scientists and specialists. The majority of such measures were addressed to individual recipients of grants, but some of them were also spread to scientific institutions where the grantees worked at home in order to guarantee their employment after coming back home from abroad, or to improve labour conditions in these institutions, make them more attractive for the employees who did not obtain such grants and, in this manner, to soften or prevent possible social tension in such research teams.

Illustrative in this respect is the example of France which in addition to programmes of individual grants also introduced parallel programmes of material and financial support of research laboratories where grantees worked. The current programmes of grants in various OECD countries show that mobility of scientists and specialists between these states and countries of CEE and CIS exerts an essential influence on the development of economic and cultural relations between them, for example between Nordic and ex-Soviet Baltic countries, Finland and Hungary, France and Romania, thus continuing the relations traditionally shaped between them, but now under different historical conditions.

The projects and programmes of international scientific cooperation are another form of assistance to scholars and research institutions of CEE and CIS countries. One can mention, as an example, the study of permafrost effected jointly by scientists of Canada, France and Russia, the programme of ecological protection of the Baltic Sea basin and safety of nuclear reactors in this region.

Another opportunity is the use of material-and-technical base of basic research available in East-European region (e.g. research equipment in scientific centers in Russia such as nuclear research centers in Dubna, Protvino, etc.) in the interests of cooperation between scientific organizations of both East and West. This should be added by the opportunity for providing a broader and more free access of East-European scientists to unique research equipment of Western research organizations, especially international centers such as CERN. It might be efficient to pool efforts of Western countries and international organizations for support and development of national R&D centers of East-European states studying unique scientific objects ("centers of excellence"), e.g. Lake Baikal in Siberia, Russia.

At the same time, taking into consideration complicated problems of reindustrialization now facing many CEE and CIS countries, West takes considerable efforts to promote applied and industrial research in post-communist countries, in particular, through the possibility of their accession to West-European programmes such as COST and EUREKA.

Experience shows that there is a number of problems which should be solved for the development of East-West cooperation for preservation and development of national R&D potentials of East-European and former USSR countries as a factor of minimization of the flow of intellectual emigration. These problems, in particular, are the following: lack of corresponding legal base in these countries and of system of information about the R&D stock of interest for Western countries, absence of data base on scientists potentially ready to go West for work or to remain home and cooperate within the framework of international projects while working at laboratories of their countries; uncertainty of intellectual property protection rights, as well as a number of other problems such as lack of guarantees from political risks, excessive taxation of research organizations, tax holidays, repatriation of profits, etc.

In the opinion of OECD experts, progress in solution of these and similar problems could substantially encourage Western participation in providing support to R&D structures in countries of CEE and CIS and in control of "brain drain" from this region. In such participation an essential role is given, especially at the present stage of development of East-West cooperation, to a cordinated Western policy pursued within the framework of international organizations.

International organizations of the UN system (UNITAR, UNCTAD, UNESCO) pay much attention to the problem of "brain drain" on the global level. For the first time the problem was put on the UN agenda already in 1968. A special resolution on the problem was adopted by the UN Conference in 1975. Within the period of 1983-1988 UNCTAD had four sessions on the issue. Special reports "Trends and Current Situation" are prepared annually which analyze the global and regional "brain drain" situation, its present state and prospects for the future. At the present time the problem of "brain drain" takes a growing role in the activity of international organizations of the UN system.

Among them an important place belongs to UNESCO which put forward the issue of migration of high-qualification personnel already 30 years ago. At that time UNESCO, in cooperation with respective bodies of United Nations and other international and state organizations of numerous countries studied various aspects of this phenomenon in detail and worked out appropriate recommendations which were then presented at the UN Conference "Science and Technology for the Development" in February, 1963.

With the account of contemporary socio-economic and political processes ongoing in CEE and former USSR countries, UNESCO through its regional division in Europe (ROSTE) located in Venice (Italy) initiated evaluation and analysis of the current situation in the sphere of "brain drain" in the region in order to elaborate a corresponding strategy of regulation of the East-West migration of scientists and specialists.

As a result of cooperation of ROSTE with G.Gulbekyan Foundation (Portugal) a task force on "brain drain" matters was formed

(Lissabon, November 1990) consisting of representatives of countries of East and West of Europe which treated the phenomenon of intellectual emigration as a common European problem exerting a noticeable influence on the entire continent. The task force formulated the following conclusions:

- one of the main factors of exodus of scientific and engineering personnel from countries of CEE and former USSR was instability of political and socio-economic situation in them which in combination with the process of democratization and improvement of observation of human rights, especially the right for freedom of mobility of citizens, contributed to the inflow of intellectuals to countries of Western Europe and other regions of the world;
- exchanges of specialists between East and West, as well as a temporary work of East-European and former Soviet scientists and engineers abroad restrain the process of emigration for permanent residence abroad and can give mutually beneficial results, since in the short run Eastern Europe and the former USSR would face difficulties in granting the required financial, material-and-technical and information resources to their most talented and highly-qualified specialists;
- many scientists and engineers in countries of CEE and CIS leave their countries for merely economic considerations or give up their professions preferring a more profitable work in other spheres of activity - commercial and administrative structures ("internal" and external "brain drain");
- in not a distant future Europe can face intellectual and culture losses caused by exodus of intellectual elite;
- this "brain drain" cannot be stopped by merely administrative measures of a prohibiting or restricting character. For this reason, it is necessary to take all possible steps to minimize negative effects of this phenomenon by way of creating better conditions of labour and homelife of researchers at their homeland;

- a considerable inflow of scientists, engineers and other specialists to the West from East-European countries and former USSR can result in certain social tension on Western markets of labour force.

Since the phenomenon of "brain drain" takes a transnational character, it should be regarded from the regional and global perspectives which enhances the role of regional and international organizations in resolving the emerging problems, in elaboration of measures for neutralization of negative effects of the "brain drain" problem.

The above-mentioned task force was an initiator of the project "Brain Drain Issues in Europe". Then a special workshop was organized (Venice, November 1991) which elaborated a methodology of studying this problem for countries of European region during the period of 1988-1993 with an obligatory disclosure of the following issues:

- analysis of political and socio-economic situation in the country;
- statistical information on the available national and regional potential of intellectual migration;
- sociological study of migration of high-qualification manpower;
- analysis of the state legislation in application to "brain drain";
- analysis of the activities of international organizations in this area;
- elaboration of measures for a comparative analysis of the positions of individual countries in respect of the "brain drain" problem, etc.

In accordance with the working plan of the special group, two international seminars on "brain drain" in Europe were organized: in Moscow in February 1992 (International seminar on "brain drain" in modern Russia: domestic and international implications) and in Warsaw in November 1992(International seminar on transformation of science in Poland: "brain drain" problem).

In April 1993 an international seminar was held in Venice under the aegis of UNESCO and its regional division ROSTE on the subject: "The "brain drain" problem in Europe". The participants worked in four sections:

- problem of "brain drain" in Europe;
- conversion of the defense sector and "brain drain";
- response of Western countries to mass emigration from CEE and former USSR;
- international organizations and "brain drain" problem.

The participants paid attention to the problem of exodus of scientific and engineering personnel from the military-industrial complex of Russia and other countries of the former USSR in connection with conversion of the military production and, accordingly, to the possibility of the appearance of nuclear and other military (chemical, biological, etc.) technologies in zones of ethnic conflicts and in possession of nationalistic and international terrorist organizations.

In the discussion of the reaction of the world community to intellectual emigration from CEE and CIS countries, it was pointed to the necessity of elaboration and implementation of concrete coordinated programmes and projects for a joint regulation of the process of "brain drain".

In February 1994 UNESCO ROSTE together with the Ministry of Science and Technological Policy of the Russian Federation organized a seminar of a group of international experts in Moscow where a report on the state, problems and prospects of "brain drain" from Russia was discussed and recommendations on possible ways of its regulation were suggested for consideration of Russian authorities responsible for elaboration and realization of the national programme of control of the "brain drain" process.

One of important initiatives of UNESCO aiming at maintenance and development of R&D potentials of CEE and CIS countries was the establishment of the Foundation of Basic Research in Russia. In March 1992 the General Director of UNESCO and President of the Russian Academy of Sciences signed an agreement and two protocols specifying the initial contribution of UNESCO to this Foundation in the amount of $300,000. [2].

UNESCO also takes efforts for improvement of the systems of higher education in countries of CEE and CIS, as well as for encouragement of elaboration of new mechanisms in the sphere of interaction between academic research institutions, universities and industry. To this end, UNESCO intends to establish a so-called "professor project" aiming at providing a stimulant international support of the reform of scientific structures in countries of the region with an accent on universities and professional communities of scholars.

As regards its concept, this project should cover nearly all disciplines of basic natural sciences. However, due to budget restrictions, it is intended to select physics as the subject of top priority. In this area a successful experience of international cooperation has been accumulated and a well-developed material base is already available in Eastern Europe. The European Physical Society (EPS) and American Physical Society (APS) are rendering now an essential aid to physicists of CEE and CIS countries and show their interest in the project, likewise international centers of physical research such as CERN in Geneva and International Center of Theoretical Physics in Triest (Italy).

It is supposed that implementation of the project would help to soften the acuity of the problem of "brain drain" from CEE countries and former USSR, to give a new impetus to research and education work in physics at universities of these countries, to attract talented young people to the science, to encourage joint research in East-West cooperation of physicists.

UNESCO also put forward an initiative of a project of East-West research-and-industrial partnership aiming at elaboration of an efficient mechanism of cooperation between universities and academic research organizations, as well as the production sector of the economy of countries of CEE and former Soviet union. The project also envisages improvement of the systems of training and re-training of research, engineering and managerial personnel. These objects are intended to accomplish by way of:

- provision of an international infrastructure to assist East-West cooperation in science and industry;
- elaboration of joint innovation projects with participation of Western companies and universities, research institutions and industrial entities of CEE and former USSR countries;
- creation of unified international standards, systems of certification and quality control of industrial products;

- assistance, to countries of the region, in their urge for adaptation of their R&D potentials to conditions of the market reform and in solving, thereby, the problem of regulation of the process of "internal" and external "brain drain".

As one of most recent actions of UNESCO aiming at expansion of East-West scientific cooperation one should mention the International Congress of managers of engineering companies and industrial leaders organized together with the International Union of Technical Organizations and Associations in Paris in June 1993. This forum formulated its object as promotion of new forms, methods and mechanisms of cooperation between universities, industrial research organizations and industry of post-communist economies under reform and of the West, integration of joint R&D projects and programmes with new systems of theoretical education and business practices of researchers, engineering and managerial personnel.

In respect of the UNESCO activity in coping with the "brain drain" problem in individual countries of CEE and the former Soviet Union, a bilateral seminar on the problem should be mentioned which was organized by UNESCO-ROSTE together with the Ministry for Science and Technological Policy in Moscow, February 21-23, 1994. The seminar was focused mainly on discussion of the report "Brain Drain" from Russia: Problems, Prospects and Ways of Regulation" prepared by a group of Russian experts under the aegis of the RF Ministry of Science and Technological Policy. The report covered such issues as the state of Russian science during the transition period, the scale and structure of migration of scientific personnel, prospects of intellectual migration from Russia and policies of countries - importers of intellectual labour force, policies of donor countries and experience of Eastern Europe, problems of state regulation and control of intellectual migration from Russia, prospects of international cooperation in solving the "brain drain" problem.

After a live discussion the participants of the seminar elaborated some recommendations for governmental authorities of Russia for consideration in making decisions relating to intellectual emigration from the country.

OECD

During recent years a great attention to the problem of "brain drain" from CEE and ex-USSR countries is paid by international community within the framework of the Organization for Economic Cooperation and Development (OECD) with its head-quarters located in Paris (France). Only during 1992-1993 under its auspices international conferences on this problem were held in France, Poland, Great Britain and Austria.

The latter conference titled "East-West Migration of Scientists and Engineers: Preservation of the Scientific and Technological Potential of the Countries of Central and Eastern Europe" had as its object an analysis of the causes, factors and conditions of the "brain drain" process, as well as evaluation of its likely post-effects on both national and international levels. It was arranged by the OECD and the Federal Ministry for Science and Research of the Republic of Austria (Vienna-Luxenburg, February 18-19, 1993).

The conference in Austria assembled about 100 heads of national departments in charge of scientific and technological development in OECD and CEE countries, immigration services, top managers and experts of international economic and scientific organizations (OECD, EU, UNESCO, UNIDO, International Organization of Migration, International Council of Scientific Unions, European Science foundation, European Academy, World Bank and some other multilateral bodies, as well as scientists and experts in scientific policy from Central and Eastern Europe (including Albania) and the former Soviet Union.

Four major topics were the focal point of discussion:

(1) the scale and structure of the flow of scientists and engineers between East and West;
(2) the problems of keeping and attracting scientists and engineers; the policies of CEE countries in this area;
(3) the encouragement of positive mobility for scientific and engineering personnel; the OECD policy on this subject;
(4) the effect of conversion of the R&D complex in the defense sector of CEE and ex-USSR countries on the international labour market of scientists and engineers.

The conference noted the inadequate terminological and methodological presentation of the problem; the absence of an appropriate statistical system for research and monitoring of the process enabling reliable international comparisons; the need for a broader international coordination and cooperation both in the research itself and in communicating its results to the attention of national and international bodies responsible for formulation of scientific and innovation policies and migration of scientists and specialists.

A great scientific event was the international conference on science, technology and innovation policies in Russia organized by the OECD together with the Ministry of Science and Technological Policy of the Russian Federation in Moscow, September 21-13, 1993. The conference gathered top-level representatives of the OECD, delegations of respective administrative bodies and academic institutions of OECD countries, top executives of Russian ministries of science and technological policy, industrial policy, other governmental offices and agencies dealing with R&D, innovation and migration in Russia.

The main topic of discussion was an evaluation report prepared by a group of experts from the OECD countries and coordinated by the OECD Secretariat on the request of the Minister for Science and Technological Policy of the Russian Federation. The document "Science, Technology and Innovation Policies: Federation of Russia. Evaluation Report" was aimed at the assessment, by a group of independent experts, of the present state and prospects of development of the Russian national R&D potential on the basis of domestic and external sources, including such important topics as R&D financing, material and technical base, obtained scientific and technological results and their use in the national economy, personnel issue with the regard of its reduction due to structural transformations, conversion of the military-industrial complex, outflow of scientists and specialists to commercial and administrative structures in the country and emigration abroad; national efforts and international assistance in preservation of Russian science. In particular, it was mentioned that (according to minimum estimation) within the framework of the bilateral national government S&T collaboration with Russia some selected OECD countries allocated the following finances, $US mln.:

Country	1992	1993
France	22	22
Germany	45	66
Japan	7	36
USA	54	228
Canada	25	25
UK	2	2
Finland	6	6
TOTAL	161	385

Source: International Cooperation of Selected OECD Countries with Russia in the Field of Science and Technology. Overview. International conference on science, technology and innovation policies in Russia, Moscow, September 21-23, 1993, p.6.

The conference came to the conclusion that a broad internationalization of Russian science and technology is the best factor for ensuring survival of their most successful constituents. Direct foreign participation can select Russian R&D institutions, teams and companies that could be efficiently integrated into the world scientific community. This internationalization facilitating transition to a market economy stipulates the following measures:

- Making easier the acquisition, distribution and use of foreign funds intended for the R&D sphere with the view to eliminating unreasonable taxes collected now and establishing a special international fund for financing Russian science and innovation structures;
- Continuous implementation of measures directed to prevention of "brain drain" from Russia through realization of cooperation projects (joint research, training of Russian specialists abroad, invitation of Russian professors and students to foreign universities, organization of various international seminars, courses, etc. in Russia);
- Ensuring support necessary for preservation of the infrastructure of science (libraries, unique research installations, computer networks) and development of material assistance to industrial research, etc.

EUROPEAN UNION (EU) (until recently European Community) and other European integration structures - international organizations (such as Commission of European Communities [CEC]) take a substantial part in rendering assistance to countries of CEE and former Soviet Union in keeping up and developing their national R&D potentials.

Relations in the sphere of science and technology between EU and CEE countries are maintained within the framework of a technical assistance (PHARE programme for CEE countries and TACIS programme for the former Soviet Union) and through scientific-and-technological cooperation in the full sense of the word - participation in actions of so-called Third Framework Programme including COST Programme, as well as proposals of CEC of April 30, 1992 on cooperation in nuclear safety, as well as activities of the International Association for Cooperation with Scientists of the ex-USSR.

These two types of relations in the R&D sphere - assistance and cooperation - mutually complement each other, though differ in methods of their realization.

In the case of a technical assistance the recipient country prepares an indicative programme of measures to be taken in the course of reforms of its economy. After examination of this programme by the CEC, with its accord and under its control each recipient country initiates a practical implementation of the assistance measures. In 1992 the PHARE programme budget was 1,000 mln. ecu and that of TACIS - 400 mln. ecu. For 1993 it was intended to allocate 1,100 mln. and 510 mln. ecu respectively. [3].

Scientific cooperation, in turn, is governed by the principle of mutual benefit stipulating, in particular, carrying out joint research by scientific organizations of EU and CEE countries, as well as equivalent exchanges of scientists and specialists.

As regards technical assistance, by February 15, 1993 only 5 countries of the region of CEE decided to allocate a part of the PHARE funds for R&D purposes: Hungary (13 mln. ecu), Poland (1 mln. ecu), Slovenia (1.6 mln. ecu), former Czechoslovakia (1 mln. ecu) and Romania (1 mln. ecu). [4]. These sums are intended mainly for carrying out organizational measures for restructuring of the mechanism of science management, upgrading scientific infrastructure, etc. A number of scientific projects (about 20 in total) are included in regional or industrial subprograms of PHARE.

Scientific-and-technological cooperation of EU with CEE countries started with a test action "PECO 92" with the total budget of

55 mln. ecu. Out of this money 40 mln. ecu were intended for scientific cooperation between EU and CEE countries, 10 mln. ecu - for participation of scientists from CEE countries in some research programmes of EU and 5 mln. ecu - for their participation in the COST programme. A tender was announced for getting this money in which 11 countries took part. After an appropriate assessment the Commission recognized 3,400 proposals as deserving financial support on the part of EU. In accordance with availability of funds in the budget 3,000 proposals are financed from 1992 budget. This money is used for granting 2,500 stipends, organization of 46 communication networks of scientific information, carrying out 160 scientific seminars and funding of 30 joint research projects. [5].

In selection of cooperation areas in 1992 the priority was given to granting stipends to scientists, their participation in international exchange of information via communication networks, as well as to support in organization of international scientific conferences and other forums of scientists and specialists from countries of EU and CEE. The main part of joint research projects was financed from 1993 budget.

It should be noted that within the framework of the "PECO 92" initiative 12,000 applications (proposals) were received for implementation of cooperation projects between EU and CEE countries aiming at preservation of R&D potentials of the latter and improvement of quality of life of researchers in these countries. The total volume of the requested financing exceeded 1.7 bln. ecu, the total number of participants of the tender was over 30,000 persons. Nearly 50% of all the filed proposals related to agreements of the "Go West" type suggesting to scientists and specialists from CEE countries an opportunity of a 3-6-months" probation at universities, research centers and industrial enterprises of EU countries. About 20% of the filed proposals related to joint research projects to be implemented by pooled efforts of research organizations of countries of EU and CEE. [6].

For 1993 it was planned to allocate 46 mln. ecu for financing of the selected proposals submitted to the contest in 1992. The measures of the Third Framework Programme provided an opportunity, for the first time for CEE countries, to take part in European research projects in such areas as environment protection, biomedicine, non-nuclear energetics, safety of nuclear synthesis.

Another initiative of EU in scientific-and-technological cooperation with CEE countries was establishment of the International Center for Science and Technology in Russia together with USA and Japan. The EU contribution is 20 mln. ecu, that of USA is $20 mln., Japan - $17 mln. [7]. This center aiming at reduction of "brain drain" from the former USSR countries envisages employment of high-qualification personnel released from the military-industrial complex as a result of conversion in civil sectors of Russian economy such as environment protection, production of alternative kinds of energy, nuclear safety. The European Parliament recommended for this Center the following priority projects: improving safety of nuclear reactors, annihilation of nuclear, chemical and biological weapons, reprocessing and burial of nuclear wastes.

EU pays a great attention to a further development of scientific-and-technological cooperation with countries of the former USSR, especially with Russia, as a factor of preserving their R&D potentials and restriction of "brain drain". In December 1992 an International Association for Cooperation with Scientists of the CIS was formed. Its founders were all countries-members of EU, as well as CEC. The Secretariat of the Association is appointed by CEC. The Association is an open organization which can be joined by other countries, national and international organizations. The main form of activity of the Association will be joint research work and international exchanges of scientists and specialists.

The research budget for 1993 allocated by EU within the framework of R&D cooperation with countries of CEE and the former USSR was 55.7 mln. ecu out of which 10.7 mln. ecu were intended for a financial support of participation of research laboratories of CEE countries in five specialized programmes implemented under the Third Framework Programme of EU and open for possible participation of East-European partners.

To impart a certain political aspect to the above-mentioned cooperation, CEC decided to invite Ministers of Science and Education of CEE countries to take part in a common European forum called International Political Commission with its Secretariat located in Vienna. The Commission has its sessions twice a year. The last session was in June 1993 in Warsaw.

The European Union has established an International All-European Fund (Mitterand's Fund, 4 mln. ecu) based in Brussels. The Fund intends to grant subsidies and scholarships to individuals and teams of specialists cooperating with Western research centers in implementation of various projects, as well as to scientists of the CIS countries visiting European research institutions. More than 90% of this aid is expected to be channelled to Russia.

Many specialized research organizations of Western Europe being preoccupied with the problem of "brain drain" from countries of CEE and former Soviet Union have substantially enlarged their R&D cooperation with these states. Among such organizations the following worth mention:

CERN

Since 1989 CERN (Centre de la Recherche Nucleaire, Geneva, Switzerland) called for a broader participation of scientists from countries of CEE and ex-USSR in its research programmes and became a sponsor of a number of scientific projects within the framework of a so-called European initiative. Poland, Czechoslovakia and Hungary were admitted to CERN as its members in December 1990, December 1991 and June 1992 respectively. It was decided that their financial contribution will be gradually growing over the period of 8 years to a full amount of a member's fee defined in per cent of their gross national product.

In June 1991 the status of an observer was given to Russian Federation. That same year Russia and CERN signed an agreement on cooperation in elaboration of a Russian accelerator and on participation of Russian scientists in the programme on safety of nuclear reactors.

CERN has been cooperating with Russian specialists in nuclear physics for quite a long time. Presently, about 100 scientists from Russia are involved in the Center's programs. About 40 of them work in Geneva and are paid by CERN. The Center maintains close relations with the International Center of Nuclear Research Institute in Dubna (near Moscow). In 1993, these two organizations concluded an agreement on cooperation and set up a coordinating committee. They plan to raise salaries of the Dubna Center personnel and renew the research equipment and instrumentation.

EUROPEAN PHYSICAL SOCIETY (EPS)

In this organization an East-West Coordination Committee was established in 1990 for coordination of scientific-and-technological cooperation of physicists from CEE, former USSR and Western Europe. EPS suggested such joint projects as creation of a common European data base on physicists, a computer communication network as a part of a system of scientific information in physical research in Europe and of exchange of this information between countries - members of EPS; organization of regular exchanges of students, post-graduates and young scholars between countries of CEE, former USSR and centers of physical research in Western Europe; creation of a common library fund (especially magazines) in physics for simplification of international exchanges with magazines and other information on physics between libraries; preparation of a data base on research equipment and unique instrumentation for physical research available in scientific organizations of Europe with the view to making easier an access to it for all interested scientists and specialists in experimental physics.

A special programme "Magazines for Russia" was initiated to provide information for organizations engaged in research in physics in countries of the former USSR, Russia in particular. It covers 20 titles of physical magazines and journals issued by 7 known publishers and is addressed to 45 centers, laboratories and institutes engaged in scientific activity in physics, as well as to certain libraries and information centers in Russia and some other CIS countries. [8].

EUREKA

A certain initiative for cooperation with countries of the former Soviet Union and CEE was demonstrated by a comprehensive European R&D Programme EUREKA. If previously the issue of participation of these countries in EUREKA projects even was not put on the agenda, in the beginning of the 90's (with the decomposition of COMECON and breakup of the Soviet Union) the programme managers revised their position. In May 1992 Hungary was admitted to EUREKA. In the second half of 1992 a special working committee was formed for relations between EUREKA and European countries - non-members of this organization.

At the 11-th Conference of EUREKA in Paris on the ministerial level on June 24, 1993 Russia was announced a member of the Programme. As it was noted at the Conference, Russian participation in EUREKA will hinder "brain drain" from Russia and will provide the required interest and prospects of scientific activity for Russian researchers and specialists at their homeland. [9].

NATO

Within the framework of NATO research programme functioning since 1958 the Research Committee of the Organization initiated two programmes of cooperation with countries of CEE and the former USSR, namely: programme of international scientific exchange and "Science for Stability" programme. The former relates to individual scientists and specialists from East-European region. It provides an opportunity of training courses in the West through various stipends, scholarships, grants or fully financing their participation in international conferences, seminars and other scientific events in Western Europe. The latter programme supporting, as a rule, applied research is intended to assistance to R&D activities directly in countries with reformed economies. Up to 30% of this scientific programme is delivered by NATO to funding of scientific organizations and projects aiming at a closer integration of scientists from countries of CEE and the former Soviet Union into the world scientific community.

At the present time, subject to the decision of the Council of the Atlantic block, programmes of the NATO Science Committee are opened for participation of scientists from CEE and the former Soviet Union countries, including Russia. This participation is effected in the following forms:

- Institutions of higher education and research organizations can take part in the programmes of intensive learning, programmes of visits of experts and programmes of support of international contacts.

Intensive learning programmes stipulate organization of scientific courses in countries of Central and Eastern Europe where lectures are delivered by leading researchers and professors from NATO countries (course duration varies from one week to one month).

The programmes of visits of experts envisages carrying out scientific examination in research organizations of CEE countries by top specialists from NATO countries sharing their professional knowledge and expertise with local experts in evaluation of major programmes and projects of scientific, technological and economic development of post-communist states. The duration of such visits also varies from several days to several weeks.

The programme of support of scientific contacts is intended to encourage expansion of relations between research teams engaged in elaboration and implementation of joint R&D projects in countries of NATO and CEE.

- Individual scientists from countries of CEE and the former Soviet Union can take part in educational programmes, programmes for arrangement of scientific seminars, as well as to receive grants for carrying out joint research.

The NATO Science Committee organized a number of international conferences on the development of the R&D sphere in Russia during the period of transition to a market economy with the focus on such problems as:

- progress of applied and industrial sciences under market-economy conditions;
- commercialization of the results of research activity and promotion of innovation in both state and private sectors of national economy;
- new forms and methods of management in the R&D sphere;
- Western experience in R&D financing and management and possibilities of its use in Russia;
- external and internal "brain drain" in Russia, its national and international implications;
- integration of educational, research and innovative activities and possible mechanisms for its realization;
- reproduction of scientific cadres and problems of employment of young scholars and specialists in view of the present state of Russian R&D sphere.

Recommendations and proposals worked out at these conferences were submitted to governmental authorities of Russian Federation responsible for scientific and technological policies.

At present the NATO Committee for Science and Technology has its representation office in Moscow. After accession of Russia to the NATO initiative "Partnership for Peace" in June 1994 a further expansion of cooperation between Russia and NATO member countries in the R&D sphere, as well as in coping with the "brain drain" problem could be expected.

EUROPEAN ACADEMY

This organization located in Berlin, Germany, has taken a series of initiatives for keeping the flow of intellectual emigrants from CEE and ex-USSR countries within reasonable limits tolerable for Germany. It elaborates and implements the programmes which enable scientists and specialists of these countries to continue their research and design work on a high level at universities and research centers of the West without breaking ties with their homeland.

Other international organizations such as European Space Agency, European Organization on Astronomy, International Center of Theoretical Physics and International Center for Science and Technology (both institutions in Triest, Italy) also expand their cooperation with research bodies of CEE and former USSR. Recently a new organization was established under the aegis of UNESCO-ROSTE - European Institute for East-West Cooperation headed by Nobel laureate Prof.Ilya Prigozhin. This institution is specially designed for R&D cooperation with Russia and some other CIS states. Of course, it is quite clear that many other international scientific organizations not mentioned above are engaged in a more or less active cooperation with R&D institutions of countries of CEE and ex-USSR aiming at helping them to cope with the "brain drain" problem.

It should be noted that international financial organizations such as World Bank, International Monetary Fund and European Bank for Reconstruction and Development also take part, though implicitly, in resolving the "brain drain" problem in countries of CEE and the former Soviet Union. Thus, during the visit of Russian Prime-Minister V.Chernomyrdin to the USA in June 1994 it was reconfirmed that the World Bank would allocate $820 mln. promised a year ago in Tokyo to Russia within the second half of 1994. The IMF provided $300 mln. for repair of Russian highways, $200 mln. for modernization of Russian banking system, $240 mln. for the development of private farms and $80 mln. - for realization of measures associated with the agrarian reform. [10]. All this will help Russia to create new jobs for its scientists, engineers and other specialists to keep them at home and thus prevent from undesirable emigration abroad.

Analysis of the stand of the above-mentioned and some other international organizations on the problem of "brain drain" from countries of CEE and the former Soviet Union shows that despite measures taken by Western countries on individual or coordinated multilateral levels in respect of endorsement of more strict requirements in their immigration legislation, introduction of more severe norms regulating the inflow of strangers from East-European region for permanent residence, two positive approaches to intellectual emigration from that region can be observed.

First of all, according to the position held by international organizations, basic efforts of both EEC and ex-USSR states themselves and of the entire global scientific community should be focused on a maximum possible preservation of their R&D potentials by way of allocation of greater resources to the sphere of science and technology, both domestic ones (state and private) and external (money from foreign national and international scientific foundations, organizations, individual private companies and physical entities, etc.), for creation of decent conditions of labour and homelife for domestic scientists and specialists and, accordingly, for solution of the existing political, ethnic and socio-economic problems for these purposes.

Secondly, international organizations take efforts for improvement of legal, organizational and economic mechanisms of integration of scientists and specialists from countries of Central and Eastern Europe and the former USSR into the international scientific community by way of encouraging exchanges of scientific ideas, information and people between East and West in the interests of the global progress of science and technology.

3.5. RUSSIA'S ATTITUDE TO INTERNATIONAL ASSISTANCE TOWARDS A SOLUTION TO THE "BRAIN DRAIN" PROBLEM

In Russia Western aid intended to preserve its national intellectual potential in general and minimize "brain drain" in particular is received with mixed feelings. On the one hand, it is quite clearly understood that under the present very severe socio-economic conditions and uncertain political situation, external assistance to Russian science and technology becomes a decisive factor of its survival and maintenance and, in some cases, even of its further development. In this sense Russia welcomes such international assistance and takes all possible measures for its better accumulation, distribution and utilization, both by the state, regional and local authorities, individual research institutions and scientists. On the other hand, it is felt that this aid could entail some internal and external problems.

Proponents of the doctrine of "technological security" of Russia hold that the West, through its mass-scale infusion of capital into the Russian R&D sphere, can divert a significant part of Russia's scientific and technological potential from the pressing national economic, scientific and technological problems, to set up inside Russia a kind of a whole R&D sector that would gear its products to the needs of progress of Western science and technology, economy in general. "He who pays the piper, calls the tune". They also say that in view of the volume of the present Western aid to Russia's science amounting to $600 mln. (or more than 1.2 trln. roubles at the exchange rate of the US dollar as of July 1994 compared to Russia's 1994 federal budget expenditures for basic research and support of scientific and technological progress of 5.048 trln.roubles [11]) there is a chance of hindering and even blocking the development of whole areas of Russian science and engineering, especially where the achievements are likely to be competitive in the world market of products manufactured on their basis.

Academician A.Baev, a well-known Russian scientist, writes, in particular: "US and EC aid to individual Russian scientists and involvement of the latter in foreign research cannot be regarded as a purely humanitarian act. This is a harsh, selfish policy, a sort of "Greek gift". What is most dangerous is that this policy leads to a personal dependence of our scientists on foreign employers. An employer-employee system of relations then follows". [12].

This point of view is, to a certain extent, not unreasonable. Having collected and processed sophisticated detailed question-naires with all the data about applicants for grants and other sub-sidies given by foreign institutions, foundations and companies, the latter possess a unique and comprehensive information on the state of research and development in Russia, the situation in individual research institutes, laboratories, etc., on the most promising and productive scientists and specialists, as well as talented students and post-graduates.

The proponents of the "technological security" doctrine hold that this information is even more valuable than that picked up by intel-ligence services and industrial espionage agents and in this sense the foreign assistance is an open and legal channel for leakage of in many cases secret information which enables foreign analysts and decision-makers to take respective political, diplomatic and eco-nomic measures against Russia, especially in the areas where it can be competitive in the world markets, thus making harm to Russia's national security interests. Besides, the scientific and technical in-formation collected in this manner can be arranged by Western counterparts into data bases and technology banks which could be operatively and efficiently used to their benefit owing to a greater production and financial potential so that Russia will be bound to buy in the future its own R&D achievements materialized by the West in respective technologies and products.

Rendering assistance to science of Russia and other CIS coun-tries even out of the most noble motives, the West is, nevertheless, far from being altruistic. Our foreign partners aim at obvious eco-nomic benefits: they capitalize on substantial savings on training the respective personnel, development of the required material-and-technical base and, mainly, on labour costs. According to the avail-able data, the pay of Russian scientists working in the West is by 4-6 times lower than that of their local colleagues at the same level of qualification and same professional duties. When working in Russia to fulfill foreign orders, Russian scientists receive 60-100 times less in hard currency than their Western counterparts. For example, un-der contracts with American Corning Glass Corporation for re-search in fibre optics Russian scientists are paid their present salaries plus about $40 extra a month ($500 a year), whereas American specialists have salaries of $70,000 and more a year for a similar job. [12].

On the other hand, foreign currency obtained by Russian scientists and specialists in the form of Western grants and other allowances engenders social tension in teams of researchers, putting whole research centers and institutes in socially unequal conditions. In quest for salaries paid in foreign currencies, against the background of an acute shortage of home investments in science and technology, many scientists and teams of researchers are ready to give away abroad valuable R&D achievements, virtually dirt-cheap. Sometimes, these are state-of-the-art developments which constitute the true national wealth of Russia. This phenomenon, some adepts of the "technological security" doctrine argue, is particularly dangerous in the R&D sphere of the military-industrial complex and in this case the country's defense potential is at stake.

Coupled with a still unrestrained "brain drain", they hold, such situation opens to the West a substantially free access to the latest achievements of Russia's scientific and technological potential, allowing the West to make an efficient use of the acquired intellectual product which in fact means, from the general economic standpoint, an overflow to the West of a fair share of Russia's national wealth without an equivalent compensation.

Thus, the problem of foreign aid and its benefit to Russian science and technology is not as simple as it may seem at first glance and the response to it in Russia is not unambiguous. A complex international approach is required to find an effective solution.

In this context, it seems reasonable to establish in Russia a government-controlled body or a public organization for coordination of international material and technical assistance to Russian science for the purpose of its more efficient distribution and use.

It is also expedient to arrange an appropriate scheme of coordination (on a multilateral basis) of the international community's efforts with the view to preserving and promoting Russian R&D potential which could include an international information system in this area, a common financial foundation or an international bank, an insurance company, etc. This would simplify the access to the foreign aid, making it more just and efficient in the interests of the entire Russian science, not of any isolated part of it.

REFERENCES

Section 3.1 & 3.2

1. D.Bobeva. Emigration of Scientists and Engineers from Bulgaria. OECD, International Conference "East-West Mobility of Scientists and Engineers", Vienna, February 18-19, 1993, pp.5-6.
2. I.Teplan. Some New Characteristics of the "Brain Drain" Process in Hungary after 1989., OECD Conference, Vienna, 1993, pp.2-3.
3. The "Brain Drain" in Poland. University of Warsaw, European Institute for regional and Local Development. Warsaw, 1992, p.38.
4. Z.Mikulova. Some Remarks on the Scientists and Engineers Mobility Activities in the Slovak Republic. OECD Conference, Vienna, 1993, p.3.
5. D.D.Palade. Some Aspects of the Mobility and "Brain Drain" in the Field of Research in Romania. OECD Conference, Vienna, 1993, p.2.
6. A.Yossifov. Bulgarian Science on the Verge of "Collapse". Emigration Flows and Their Impact on Bulgarian Science. Supplement. UNESCO-ROSTE International Conference on "Brain Drain " Issues in Europe. Venice, April 1993., p.5.
7. D.Bobeva, op.cit., pp.7-8.
8. I.Teplan,op.cit.
9. Roumanie, Ministere de la Recherche et de la Technologie, La Conference Est-Ouest por la Mobilite, Vienne, 18-19 Fevrier 1993, p.8.
10. I.Teplan, op.cit.
11. The "Brain Drain" in Poland..., pp.73-74.
12. I.Teplan, op.cit.
13. D.D.Palade, op.cit.

Section 3.3

1. Statement by the Federal Ministry of Education and Science of the Federal Republic of Germany, OECD Vienna Conference on mobility of scientists and engineers between East and West. February 18-19, 1993.
2. East-West Mobility of Scientists and Engineers. Paper by the UK delegation. OECD Vienna Conference, February 18-19, 1993.
3. Maintaining the Scientific and Technological Potential of CEE Countries. Vienna Conference, February 18-19, 1993.
4. Mobility of Scientists and Engineers between Italy and CEE Countries. OECD Vienna Conference, February 18-19, 1993.
5. Mobility of Scientists and Engineers between Netherlands and CEE Countries. Policies, Programmes and Figures. OECD Vienna Conference, February 18-19, 1993.
6. Norwegian R&D and CEE Countries. OECD Vienna Conference, February 18-19, 1993.
7. Mobility of Researchers between Finland and CEE countries. OECD Vienna Conference, February 18-19, 1993.
8. Herald of the Russian Academy of Sciences, 1993, vol.63, No.4, p.313.
9. Programmes of Scientific Exchanges Between Japan and Countries of Central and Eastern Europe. OECD Vienna Conference, February 18-19, 1993., p.3.
10. ITAR-TASS Information, AM-series, December 15, 1993, pp.6-7.
11. KOMPAS (Bulletin of Printed Information), INO TASS, September 9, 1991, No. 175, p.11.
12. USAID Fact Sheet, Washington, April 1993, No.93-8.
13. "Finansovye Izvestiya" ("Financial News"), No. 28, May 8-14, 1993, p.1.
14. USAID Fact Sheet, April 1993, No.93-12.
15. Ibid., No.93-16.
16. Ibid., No.93-20.
17. "Poisk" ("Search"), No. 23, June 10-16, 1994, p.11.
18. Guide to Programs Fiscal Year 1994. National Science Foundation, 1994, pp. 81-82.
19. Herald of the Russian Academy of Sciences, Vol.63, No.9, 1993, p.650.
20. New York Times. Weekly Review. February 2-15, 1993, pp. B1-B2 (in Russian).

21. "Izvestiya", April 6, 1994.
22. "Izvestiya", May 31, 1994.

Section 3.4 & 3.5

1. "Izvestiya", November 30, 1992.
2. M.Abtahi. A brief summary of UNESCO activities. OECD Vienna Conference "East-West Mobility of Sceintists and Engineers", February 18-19, 1993, p.4.
3. Scientific and technological relations between the European Community and countries of Central and Eastern Europe. Commission of the European Communities, Brussels, February 16, 1993, p.1.
4. Ibid., p.2.
5. Ibid., p.3.
6. G.Carante. Scientific international organizations and their contributions to the brain-drain issues. UNESCO-ROSTE International Seminar on Brain-Drain Issues in Europe, April 25-27, 1993, Venice, Italy, p.4.
7. Ibid., p.5.
8. European Physical Society. Report on the Activities of the East-West Coordination Committee in 1992. UNESCO-ROSTE International Seminar on Brain-Drain Issues in Europe, April 25-27, Venice, Italy, pp.11, 13-14.
9. "Izvestiya" June 26, 1993.
10. "Izvestiya" June 25, 1994.
11. "Rossijskiye Vesti", July 6, 1994, p.4.
12. "Poisk", 1993, No.7, pp.12,18.
13. "New York Times. Weekly Reviw", June 9-22, 1992, p.B1-B2.

CHAPTER IV

POSSIBLE WAYS OF REGULATION OF THE "BRAIN DRAIN" FROM RUSSIA

Since the problem of "brain drain" on any noticeable scale substantially did not exist for Russia when it was within the former Soviet Union due to a relatively "closed" nature of the Soviet society, no appropriate mechanism for controlling emigration of intellectuals was available. The main channel of emigration, or ethnic emigration, was controlled (in respect of necessary formalities: invitations, passports, visas, etc.) by the USSR Ministry of Interior through its Department of Visas and Registrations (OVIR), and the Main Directorate of State Customs Control under the USSR Ministry of External Economic Relations, as well as by the notorious Committee for State Security (KGB) which kept a vigilant eye on potential bearers of secrets and did not let them out of the country.

At the end of the 80's and beginning of the 90's when a considerable leap-like growth of emigration took place as a result of a profound crisis of the Soviet society and the socialist system in general, as well as liberalization of laws and procedures of exit from the country, it became clear that something should be done to cope with the "brain drain" problem, because its negative effects such as lagging-behind of some areas of domestic science and technology, shortage of professors and lecturers in educational institutions and a related threat to the system of reproduction of scientific and engineering specialists, deficit and lowered quality of medical services, etc. became noticeable.

For this reason, a group of Russian public figures most anxious with the shaping trend of exodus of intellectuals put forward the initiative of an all-round studying of the "brain drain" process, its reasons, motives and factors and making recommendations for control and regulation of intellectual emigration. On the initiative of the USSR Commission (since 1992 the Commission of Russian Federation) for the UNESCO a public organization - Russian Committee for the "Brain Drain" Problems was established in September 1991. From the very beginning of its activities the Committee initiated a broad campaign for attracting attention of both domestic and international scientific community to the problem of "brain drain" from Russia.

The Committee set up a working group which carried out a study of the available statistical information, arranged a number of sociological investigations, polling of the population and staff of some major scientific centers, analyzed the existing local and foreign literature on the problem, established links with a number of foreign research centers and international organizations.

In February 1992 the Committee organized an international seminar "Brain Drain" in Modern Russia: Internal and International Aspects (Moscow, Vatutinki). Participants of the seminar were - top-level experts in basic and applied research from the leading research centers of Russia (Moscow and Moscow region, St.-Petersburg, Novosibirsk, etc., heads of some major research institutions of the Russian Academy of Sciences (RAS), specialists from its institutes of political, economic and sociological profiles, as well as from industrial research institutes and design bureaus; researchers and professors from a number of well-known educational institutions of Russia; top executives from various ministries and agencies concerned; representatives of business circles, commercial structures and public funds; scientists and officials from the CIS countries; delegations from international organizations such as UNESCO-ROSTE, Commission of the European Communities, the World Institute of Science in Paris, and others; journalists from the leading domestic and foreign mass media agencies.

The seminar was the first major scientific and public event in Russia that put on the agenda the urgent and acute issues of intellectual emigration from this country, discussed its diverse aspects, problems and implications, elaborated some practical recommendations and submitted them to the governmental authorities of Russia and to international organizations concerned. It was a sort of a catalyst for further studies, analysis of the "brain drain" process and elaboration of some practical measures for its regulation and their implementation.

In October 1993 at the session of the RF Commission for UNESCO the Committee for the "Brain Drain" Problems was included in the list of working bodies of the Commission. The main tasks of the Committee are the following:

- organization of continuous statistical and sociological monitoring and analysis of the scale, professional structure, geographic areas of the "brain drain" process, its trends and implications and, on this basis, presentation of information to decision-making authorities and scientific community of Russia;
- coordination of activities of Russia's public and administrative organizations in overcoming negative consequences of intellectual emigration from the country, elaboration of a concept of regulation of the "brain drain" process;
- participation in preparing a Draft State Programme of "Brain Drain" Process Regulation;
- establishing contacts with foreign scientific communities and with scientists and engineers, as well as other specialists emigrated from Russia and now living abroad;
- rendering assistance to Russian emigrant scientists and specialists, including those who would like to come back home;
- analysis, publication and dissemination of information on the problems of intellectual emigration;
- participation in realization of the UNESCO project "Brain Drain in Europe.

Parallel to, and in many cases owing to, the activities of the public Russian National Committee on Brain Drain Problems many administrative structures became involved in solution of this problem. Among them the following organizations should be mentioned: RF Ministry of Science and Technological Policy (which is an informal coordinator of activities in this area and) where the Department of Social Problems of Science initiated the work on elaboration of a state programme for regulation of intellectual emigration from Russia and presented its own draft of this programme; Federal Migration Service, Federal Employment Service, RF Ministry of Interior,

RF Ministry of Labour, Ministry of Foreign Affairs, RF State Customs Committee, RF State Committee for Higher Education, Russian Academy of Sciences, RF Ministry for Social Protection of the Population, RF State Committee for Statistics. Certain work is being done at the President Administration, RF State Committee for Defense Industries, RF Ministry for Cooperation with Member States of the CIS, and in some other governmental bodies.

However, since no comprehensive concept of the "brain drain" process regulation has been elaborated so far, their efforts are not properly coordinated, are fragmented and not interrelated, so that no adequate tangible practical measures have been elaborated and implemented in this area.

In our opinion, the concept and programme of "brain drain" regulation should be worked out as an immanent integral part of the general concept of Russia's national-state interests, its national security, strategy of socio-economic and political development, regional, demographic and ethnic policies, international relations.

In this broad context, competent parliament and government bodies of Russia should formulate, above all, a concept, strategy and a respective mechanism for national scientific and technological development based on an optimal use of domestic and external sources. Priorities should be given to mobilization of Russia's own resources, more sizeable and efficient state support of national R&D potential, creation of adequate labour and social conditions for scientists and specialists preventing them from undesirable exodus both abroad and to sectors of national economy unconnected with scientific creative activity.

The policy of "brain drain" regulation should be based not on the principle of minimization of the emigration flow (which in fact would mean restrictive and prohibitive measures, i.e. return to the former totalitarian system and violation of human rights and freedoms), but on the principle of minimization of losses brought by "brain drain" to Russia's national economy by way of a purposeful influence on the entire complex of motives, reasons, factors and conditions of the emigration process within the framework of a state strategy.

This strategy should be reflected in a specific programme of regulation of intellectual emigration comprising a comprehensive system of mutually interrelated and balanced measures of organizational, legal, institutional and socio-economic character designed both for the current period and the medium-term and long-term perspective, tightly interwoven with the general policy of scientific-and-technological and socio-economic development of Russia.

In view of the foregoing, it is an object of a purported state programme of regulation of intellectual emigration to minimize damages to the national economy resulting from exodus of scientists and specialists, to compensate these damages through the economic effect obtained from labour migration abroad, scientific-and-technological and economic cooperation with intellectual diaspora of former fellow countrymen abroad and with international scientific community.

The programme's task is to provide a rational mechanism of control and regulation of the "brain drain" process and creation of appropriate conditions for its efficient functioning.

The programme should be oriented mainly on high-qualification personnel constituting elite of intellectual potential of the society and ensuring its reproduction. The programme relates to that part of the intellectual socium which is concentrated mainly in the R&D sphere, though it is also intended for the people engaged in other spheres of intellectual creative activity (culture, arts, education, medicine, etc.).

The mechanism of implementation of the programme should consist of a complex of leverage of legal, institutional, economic and social nature and two interrelated blocks - internal and international.

The mode of reduction of the programme to practice has a multi-level character (federal, sectoral, regional, municipal, level of separate institutions and individual scientists and specialists) and comprises a combination of concerted efforts of state, public and private entrepreneurial structures.

On the state level a strategy of socio-economic development is defined along with the objectives, tasks and mechanism of national scientific and technological policy, role and place of intellectual emigration in it and basic parameters of its regulation.

On the regional level particular measures are elaborated with the due account of economical-and-geographic specificity of a region, its specialization in national R&D, concentration of scientific personnel. These measures are aimed mainly at creation of decent labour and homelife conditions, other economic incentives, social protection of scientists and specialists with the view to retaining them at home so as to optimize migration and emigration flows.

On the sectoral level, with the account of specific areas of some basic and applied research (nuclear physics, nuclear engineering, certain fields of R&D associated with the military-industrial complex, chemistry and biotechnology, etc.) special measures are worked out for protection of national defense interests, as well as international security interests of the world community, and appropriate conditions for labour migration and emigration are defined.

On the level of research centers, design offices, educational institutions and other scientific organizations appropriate steps are taken to keep up already existing scientific schools, to match their research and educational functions and efforts with the changing priorities of national socio-economic development, new trends in the world science and technology so as to effect a better planning of domestic and international scientific cooperation, exchanges of scientists and specialists both within the country and outside it, thus optimizing labour migration and emigration flows.

On the level of individual scientists and specialists this policy supposes elaboration of a respective mechanism of observation of the entire complex of human rights and freedoms, as well as obligations and duties of a citizen involved in the emigration process in respect of home and host country with the due account of both national and international laws, rules and procedures.

For a better coordination of studies of the "brain drain" process and its practical regulation, it seems expedient to organize, under the RF Security Council or at the RF Ministry of Science and Technological Policy, an All-Russian scientific-coordination Council for research into the problem of intellectual emigration according to an agreed concept and a unified programme of interaction of state, public (including the RF National Committee for the "Brain Drain" Problems) and other organizations concerned.

It is also advisable to assess the real scale of exodus of scientific and engineering personnel from Russia, its qualification-professional structure, geographic directions, actual damage to the national economy on the basis of a specially designed system of internationally accepted and comparable statistical indicators, forms of statistical observation and reporting with interaction of the RF Committee for Statistics, RF Ministry of Interior, other agencies and offices related to the problem of migration and emigration. It would be of interest to draw up, on the basis of the thus-obtained information, a sort of a regional "brain-drain" map of Russia enabling a proper apprehension of regional pattern and trends of intellectual exodus, its structural and geographic character, territorial and local specificity, so as to reasonably formulate appropriate federal and regional socio-economic, scientific-and-technological, demographic, labour and ethnic policies in the future.

It seems desirable to prepare alternative forecasts (for different scenarios of political and socio-economic development of Russia) of intellectual emigration from this country for the short-run and medium-term perspective in comparison with respective estimates of the capacity of the international market of intellectual labour in respect of its possible absorption of the scientific and engineering personnel emigrating from Russia so as to get ready for working out appropriate measures for employment of the excessive number of potential emigrants.

A unified state data base (register) of scientists and specialists going abroad from Russia for a temporary work or for permanent residence and already working abroad could be formed at the RF State Committee for Statistics or under the RF Ministry of Science and Technological Policy, as well as appropriate data bases for potential vacancies for scientists and engineers in Russia and abroad.

As regards measures of a legal character relating to regulation of the "brain drain" process, it would be expedient:

- to sign a series of bilateral international agreements on migration of scientific and engineering personnel between Russia and foreign countries concerned or to include respective sections or provisions into already existing agreements and treaties on ethnic and labour migration of the population; to join or ratify the existing multilateral international agreements on emigration matters;

- to work out a procedure for going abroad for a permanent and temporary work of Russian scientists and specialists subject to the norms of the RF Law on Entry and Exit and respective international rules and practices;

- to elaborate the order of employment of scientific and engineering personnel coming back to Russia from abroad after completion of education, post-graduate course, professional training and work on a contract;

- to provide a system of legislative and normative acts regulating scientific-and-technological and business cooperation of Russian scientists and specialists with emigrants - former Soviet nationals - both in Russia and

abroad; for promotion of such cooperation, it would be desirable to envisage preferential conditions of taxation, crediting, trade and customs tariffs and rules, simplified visa formalities;
- to assist realization of the initiative of some foreign countries for establishment, in Russia and abroad, of international centers, funds, programmes and projects for support of Russian science and regulation of the "brain drain" from Russia by way of signing appropriate international agreements.

Of course, the above-mentioned and similar measures can be regarded as the follow-up of respective legal measures of a broader scope generally relating to the development of Russian science and technology.

To preserve and revitalize Russian science potential, it is advisable to adopt a package of laws, in particular:

- on the state scientific and technological policy,
- on the Russian Academy of Sciences,
- on an academic research institution,
- on the status of a researcher,
- on protection of intellectual property, state scientific and technological secrets and "know how",
- on transfer of technology on international and national levels including spinoff from defense industries to civil ones,
- on science cities so as to combine and interrelate interests of the state, regions, municipal authorities, research collectives and to ensure a balanced development of national science and technology in individual regions, etc.

As regards the block of economic measures to be taken within the framework of a mechanism for regulation of the "brain drain" process, also within a broader context of socio-economic transformations aiming at elevation of living standards in Russia, provision of better labour and homelife conditions for its scientists and specialists, the following steps could be suggested.

First of all, it is highly desirable to establish a system of following the trends of development in world science and technology, to determine the place occupied by Russian R&D potential in this process in order to elaborate and implement a scientifically substantiated state policy of Russia in science and technology.

It is also advisable to carry out a full-scale assessment of the accumulated stock of R&D results for their further commercialization in state and private innovation companies, both in Russia and abroad, using such forms as intellectual-property exchange markets, innovation funds, commercial investment banks, technology incubators, business "green houses", insurance and venture companies, etc., as well as appropriate credit and tax preferences for their efficient activity.

The average salary of researchers should be made at least equal to the average wage in industry; it is necessary to eliminate disproportions existing now in remuneration of intellectual labour in Russia, to elevate the social status of a scholar, engineer, inventor, professor, to make their labour, both morally and financially, equivalent to that in a civilized society.

It is about time to form a network of centers for retraining and improving qualification skills of the R&D personnel released from the sphere of science and technology as a result of restructuring, closing of research centers and institutions, conversion of the military-industrial complex and its research organizations in accordance with the needs of Russia's national economy, especially in the consumer sector, in food industry, housing, services, medical care, etc.

It is advisable to establish an All-Russian Labour Exchange Market for R&D personnel with the data bank of available vacancies in scientific and technological sphere, educational and production activities in Russia up-dated by information centers of industrial ministries and enterprises, research institutions and design offices, other organizations concerned. This Labour Exchange could function on a commercial basis in a close cooperation with the Federal Migration Service, Federal Employment Service, other related offices and agencies. It could have affiliates and divisions in major regional centers, big cities all over Russia which would be intercommunicating through a special nation-wide network. Unemployed scientists and specialists could apply for jobs to such local offices of the All-Russian Labour Exchange and the latter could assist them in finding suitable work and residence places in any region of the country and even abroad.

Material and financial incentives should be provided for promotion of scientific and innovation activities so that individual scientists and specialists, research teams, production enterprises (irrespective of forms of ownership) be interested in the development and practical use of new technologies, machinery and equipment.

In this sense, it should be reasonable to adopt appropriate rates of preferential medium- and long-term crediting of R&D from such sources as state and commercial banking institutions, investment and innovation funds, financial corporations, insurance companies, newly formed financial-industrial groupings to provide funding of specific research and innovation programs and projects selected for implementation on the basis of competition.

Maintenance of Russian R&D potential, creation of new jobs for scientists and specialists could be also encouraged by a rational taxation policy stipulating respective preferences for enterprises and organizations creating and implementing new technologies and industrial products. They should be given the opportunity of using tax holidays, especially in the initial period of their existence, or during the stage of starting up and commissioning of new plants, shift to the manufacture of new products; special free entrepreneurial and technological zones should be arranged to serve as "tax oasises" for attraction of state and private capital investments in national R&D and innovation activities.

From the economic standpoint it seems advantageous to initiate and develop scientific-and-technological and economic cooperation with former fellow countrymen living now abroad. An important precondition for a successful work in this direction could be formation of a data bank on intellectual emigrants using a respective system of statistical observation reflecting their present residence, professional occupation in a certain sector of national economy of the host country (science, business, civil service, etc.) in order to reveal promising and advantageous areas of a further efficient cooperation on a mutually beneficial basis, in particular for attraction of emigrants' capital, technologies, expertise to the economy of Russia and other countries of the former USSR.

As regards intellectuals leaving Russia through the channels of labour migration, the effect of compensation of their temporary exclusion from Russia's national economy could be achieved at the account of direct fiscal measures (charging taxes and fees from incomes of the migrants and their foreign employers, etc.) and indirect profits resulting from their improved knowledge, qualification level, professional skills acquired during their stay abroad and realized in Russia after coming back home.

Measures for social protection of scientists and specialists in Russia could include an assessment, both in scale and structure, the R&D potential released in national economy for various reasons (restructuring, conversion), to define its part potentially liable to emigration and exodus to national structures non-associated with R&D and educational activities, work out and realize a system of steps contributing to attraction of such people to small- and medium-size innovation business, retraining centers, etc., to allocate money from the state budget and other sources for welfare and other allowances to temporarily unemployed intellectuals.

Certain preferences should be also provided for the above-mentioned categories of specialists in respect of dwelling facilities for them and their families, places in nurseries, kindergartens and schools, medical services, allowances and other bonuses for medical treatment and rehabilitation. In the case of their departure abroad for a long-time temporary work, they should have the right for securing their lodging facilities, insurance of their property and the right for a residence permit in big scientific and industrial cities of Russia upon coming back home.

It is very important to take into consideration psychological stereotypes of public thinking about the role and place of science in the society and to exert a purposeful influence on them with the view to elevating the social and economic status of representatives of intellectual labour, prestige of a researcher, inventor, professor through an active propaganda of creative and inventive activity. It is desirable in this context to arrange a system of continuous information of both domestic and foreign public, through mass media, about achievements of Russian science and technology, outstanding scientists and engineers, state policy in R&D and innovation, current and future areas of application of the results of intellectual activity of scientists and specialists.

Russian public should be aware of the true situation in which our former fellow countrymen find themselves after emigration abroad, with the opportunities of scientific and business cooperation with them. For this purpose a number of international conferences with their participants could be arranged both in Russia and in major countries of immigration (USA, Germany, Israel, etc.), as well as telecommunication "bridges" and similar forms of contacts between representatives of different countries concerned. It is obvious that such information and propaganda measures could make an essential contribution to a positive solution of "brain drain" from Russia and other countries of the former USSR.

Since the problem of intellectual emigration from Russia and other CIS states has far-reaching international consequences, it should be solved within the framework of a broad international co-operation. It seems expedient that such cooperation be also spread over coordination of Western financial assistance to maintaining Russian R&D potential in the case of labour migration of Russian scientists and specialists abroad for a temporary work. In this case Western countries could accord and reasonably share quotas for Russian scientists and scholars allowed to come to them, their specialization in education and training according to requests by Russian official and private organizations, etc., preferably on the basis of a coordinated migration programme.

In the case of rendering financial assistance to Russian science, in particular by way of preserving existing jobs and creating new ones for intellectual laborers directly in Russia and other CIS countries with the view to preventing them from undesirable and excessive migration abroad, it would be advisable to establish a special international foundation.

It could be formed both out of governmental sources (budgets) of the member-countries concerned and the money allocated by international governmental and non-governmental organizations, national and international scientific foundations, other public organizations, private business structures, individual physical persons.

A function of such foundation could be, on the one hand, support of Russian science by financing individual scientists and teams of researchers, including the system of grants, promotion of international contacts, provision of research centers with the required equipment, instruments and materials, as well as foreign scientific literature, etc. On the other hand, this international foundation could render assistance to Russian scientists going abroad for a permanent or temporary work (travelling and resettlement expenses, financial support during the period of finding job, etc.). This foundation, or some other sources could allocate money to invite, on a competition basis, foreign scientists, science managers and other intellectuals to Russia to fill vacancies caused by emigration and which for some reasons cannot be occupied in the immediate future by domestic specialists. The foundation could also provide a financial support to international universities, colleges, lyceums for gifted children, summer schools for young scientists, etc. both in Russia and abroad.

It is also advisable to establish a coordinated international information service so as to better inform ex-Soviet scientific communities about the opportunities for obtaining financial support from the West, such as grant, scholarships, stipends, etc., about job opportunities abroad, various conferences and other scientific events. On the other hand, such an information system could incorporate data bases on Russian technologies of interest for implementation in the West or in Russia with foreign assistance, as well as on students, post-graduates, professors and other specialists - possible candidates for work abroad - so as to simplify the procedure of selection of proper people, make easier the formalities for their migration.

For a broader involvement of Russian and other ex-Soviet scientists and scholar into the system of foreign support, it seems advisable to extend the number of programmes of assistance to the age category of from 40 to 55 years, because this age group covers the majority of researchers, whereas the existing programmes and projects of international cooperation relate mainly to young people (below 40 years age) and scientific elite (usually above 55) so that a great number of Russian scientists and specialists find themselves outside foreign aid and this can give rise to a social discontent in the domestic scientific community. One of possible forms of such programmes could be sabbatical leaves which are totally unknown in Russian academic practice. This could be also effected through the above-mentioned international assistance foundation.

These and other similar measures could substantially alleviate the painful problem of "brain drain" from Russia and assist the country to use its scientific, technological and production potentials more fully and effectively so as to restore previous advanced positions of Russia in the world scientific community.

A N N E X

TABLE 1. STRUCTURE OF EMIGRANTS FROM RUSSIA ACCORDING TO SECTORS AND COUNTRIES, 1992, 1993

Countries	Total adult workable citizens	Sectors						
		Industry, energetics, transport, communications, material supply, construction	Agriculture, forestry, procurement	Trade, public catering, lodging and communal services, insurance, management	Science and public education	Public health, social care, sport	Culture and arts	Other activities
Total:								
1992	58730	16164	8736	4623	4572	4110	1063	19472
1993	67775	19668	9813	4765	5876	4180	1132	22341
				1-st group of countries*				
Total:								
1992	454	78	3	37	31	13	16	276
1993	395	67	3	17	38	30	9	231

Table 1 (continued)

Including:								
Poland								
1992	127	18	2	12	11	1	5	78
1993	121	13	1	6	10	8	3	80
Bulgaria								
1992	99	29	1	5	9	4	6	45
1993	105	27	0	5	13	10	2	48
Czechoslovakia								
1992	92	11	0	7	5	3	1	65
1993	45	4	0	1	4	6	2	28
Yugoslavia								
1992	58	13	0	9	2	4	4	26
1993	19	5	0	0	2	2	0	11
Other countries								
1992	78	7	0	4	4	1	0	62
1993	104	18	2	5	9	4	2	64
			2-st group of countries *					
Total:								
1992	58276	16086	8733	4586	4541	4097	1037	19196
1993	67385	19601	9810	4748	5838	4150	1123	22110

Table 1 (continued)

Including:									
Germany									
	1992	34202	10610	8455	2854	2765	2246	497	6793
	1993	43457	13866	9358	3162	3536	2508	542	10485
Israel									
	1992	13972	3355	171	1217	1163	1299	392	6375
	1993	12635	3408	297	1069	1116	902	270	5573
USA									
	1992	7964	1569	82	341	477	445	138	4912
	1993	9076	1804	88	393	939	589	270	4993
Greece									
	1992	848	357	18	107	43	65	6	252
	1993	743	258	49	61	74	58	7	236
Australia									
	1992	514	83	2	21	50	17	9	332
	1993	335	59	0	12	48	28	6	182
Finland									
	1992	214	56	1	30	15	10	3	99
	1993	300	50	10	11	26	20	9	174
Canada									
	1992	137	18	0	5	10	5	2	97
	1993	334	75	3	15	52	20	5	164
Sweden									
	1992	90	8	2	4	6	3	1	66
	1993	140	26	0	9	11	12	5	77

Table 1 (continued)

United Kingdom								
1992	37	4	1	2	4	0	0	26
1993	26	4	0	0	6	1	2	13
Italy								
1992	19	1	0	0	1	0	0	17
1993	19	2	0	1	2	0	0	14
Spain								
1992	119	6	0	1	0	2	1	109
1993	22	3	1	0	0	1	0	16
France								
1992	13	0	0	0	0	0	0	13
1993	18	2	0	2	3	0	1	10
Other countries								
1992	147	19	1	4	7	5	6	105
1993	281	50	4	13	25	11	5	173

Notes: 1-st group of countries: CEE, Baltia, countries of former Yugoslavia, former Asian socialist countries and Cuba.
2-st group of countries: capitalist and developing countries.

TABLE 2. PROPORTION OF EMIGRANTS FROM RUSSIA
FOR PERMANENT RESIDENCE ABROAD, ACCORDING TO COUNTRIES,
IN THEIR TOTAL NUMBER IN RESPECTIVE SECTORS (%), IN 1992,1993

Countries		Total adult workable citizens	Sectors						
			Industry, energetics, transport, communications, material supply, construction	Agriculture, forestry, procurement	Trade, public catering lodging and communal services, insurance, management	Science and public education	Public health, social care, sport	Culture and arts	Other activities
Total:	1992	100%	100	100	100	100	100	100	100
	1993	100%	100	100	100	100	100	100	100
1-st group of countries*									
Total:	1992	0.77	0.48	0.03	0.80	0.68	0.32	1.52	1.42
	1993	0.58	0.34	0.03	0.35	0.64	0.71	0.79	1.03
Including: Poland	1992	0.22	0.11	0.02	0.26	0.24	0.02	0.47	0.40
	1993	0.18	0.06		0.12	0.17	0.19	0.26	0.35

Table 2 (continued)

Bulgaria								
1992	0.17	0.18	0.01	0.11	0.20	0.10	0.57	0.23
1993	0.15	0.13		0.10	0.22	0.23	0.17	0.21
Czechoslovakia								
1992	0.16	0.07		0.15	0.11	0.07	0.09	0.33
1993	0.06	0.02		0.02	0.06	0.14	0.17	0.12
Yugoslavia								
1992	0.10	0.08		0.19	0.04	0.10	0.38	0.13
1993	0.02	0.02			0.03	0.04		0.04
Other countries								
1992	0.13	0.04		0.09	0.09	0.02		0.32
1993	0.15	0.09	0.02	0.10	0.15	0.09	0.17	0.28
2-st group of countries*								
Total:								
1992	99.23	99.52	99.97	99.20	9.32	99.68	98.48	98.58
1993	99.42	99.65	99.97	99.65	99.36	99.29	99.21	98.97
Including:								
Germany								
1992	58.24	65.64	96.78	61.73	60.48	54.65	45.49	34.86
1993	64.11	70.74	95.36	66.35	60.17	49.76	47.88	46.93
Israel								
1992	23.79	20.76	1.96	26.32	25.44	31.61	37.23	32.74
1993	18.66	17.32	3.02	22.43	18.99	21.57	23.85	24.97

Table 2 (continued)

USA									
	1992	13.56	9.71	0.94	7.38	10.43	10.83	13.11	25.23
	1993	13.39	9.72	0.44	8.24	15.98	14.09	23.85	22.34
Greece									
	1992	1.44	2.21	0.21	2.31	0.94	1.58	0.57	1.29
	1993	1.09	1.37	0.49	1.28	1.25	1.38	0.61	1.05
Australia									
	1992	0.88	0.51	0.02	0.45	1.09	0.41	0.85	1.71
	1993	0.49	0.29		0.25	0.81	0.66	0.53	0.81
Finland									
	1992	0.36	0.35	0.01	0.65	0.33	0.24	0.28	0.51
	1993	0.44	0.25	0.10	0.24	0.44	0.44	0.79	0.77
Canada									
	1992	0.23	0.11		0.11	0.22	0.12	0.19	0.50
	1993	0.49	0.38	0.03	0.31	0.88	0.47	0.44	0.73
Sweden									
	1992	0.15	0.05	0.02	0.09	0.13	0.07	0.09	0.34
	1993	0.20	0.13		0.18	0.18	0.28	0.44	0.34
United Kingdom									
	1992	0.06	0.02	0.01	0.04	0.09			0.13
	1993	0.03	0.02			0.10	0.02	0.17	0.05
Italy									
	1992	0.03	0.01			0.02			0.09
	1993	0.02	0.01		0.02	0.03			0.06

Table 2 (Continued)

Spain								
1992	0.20	0.04		0.02		0.05	0.09	0.56
1993	0.03	0.01	0.01			0.02	0.08	0.07
France								
1992	0.02							0.07
1993	0.02	0.01		0.04	0.05		0.08	0.04
Other countries								
1992	0.25	0.12	0.01	0.09	0.15	0.12	0.57	54.00
1993	0.40	0.25	0.04	0.27	0.42	0.26	0.44	0.77

Notes: see Annex Table 1.

TABLE 3. PROPORTION OF EMIGRANTS FROM RUSSIA
FOR PERMANENT RESIDENCE ABROAD, ACCORDING TO SECTORS (%),
IN THEIR TOTAL NUMBER FOR RESPECTIVE COUNTRIES, 1992-1993

Countries	Total adult workable citizens	Sectors						
		Industry, energetics, transport, communications, material supply, construction	Agriculture, forestry, procurement	Trade, public catering, lodging and communal services, insurance, management	Science and public education	Pubic health, social care, sport	Culture and arts	Other activities
Total:								
1992	100.0	27.5	14.9	7.9	7.8	7.0	1.8	33.2
1993	100.0	29.0	14.5	7.0	8.7	6.2	1.6	33.0
1-st group of countries*								
Total:								
1992	100.0	17.2	0.7	8.1	6.8	2.9	3.5	60.8
1993	100.0	17.0	7.0	43.0	96.0	7.5	2.3	58.6
Including:								
Poland								
1992	100.0	14.2	1.5	9.4	8.7	0.8	3.9	61.4
1993	100.0	10.7	0.8	4.9	8.2	6.6	2.4	66.4

Table 3 (Continued)

Bulgaria								
1992	100.0	29.3	1.0	0.1	9.1	4.0	6.1	45.5
1993	100.0	25.7		4.8	12.4	9.5	1.9	45.7
Czechoslovakia								
1992	100.0	12.0		1.6	5.4	3.3	1.1	70.7
1993	100.0	18.9		2.2	8.9	13.3	4.4	62.3
Yugoslavia								
1992	100.0	22.4		15.5	3.4	6.9	6.9	44.8
1993	100.0	26.3			10.5	10.5		57.8
Other countries								
1992	100.0	9.0			5.1	1.3		79.5
1993	100.0	17.3	1.9	4.8	8.7	3.9	1.9	61.5
2-st group of countries *								
Total:								
1992	100.0	27.6	15.0	7.9	7.8	7.0	1.8	32.9
1993	100.0	29.1	14.6	7.0	8.7	6.1	1.7	32.8
Including:								
Germany								
1992	100.0	31.0	24.7	8.3	8.1	6.6	1.4	19.9
1993	100.0	31.9	21.5	7.2	8.1	5.8	1.2	24.1
Israel								
1992	100.0	24.0	1.2	4.3	6.0	5.6	1.7	61.7
1993	100.0	26.9	2.4	8.5	8.8	7.1	2.1	44.2

Table 3 (Continued)

USA	1992	100.0	19.7	1.0	4.3	6.0	5.6	1.7	61.7
	1993	100.0	19.9	1.0	4.3	10.3	6.5	2.9	55.1
Greece	1992	100.0	42.1	2.1	12.6	5.1	7.7	0.7	29.7
	1993	100.0	34.7	6.6	8.2	10.0	7.8	0.9	31.8
Australia	1992	100.0	16.1	0.4	4.1	9.7	3.3	1.8	64.6
	1993	100.0	17.6		3.6	14.3	8.3	1.8	54.4
Finland	1992	100.0	26.2	0.5	14.0	7.0	4.7	1.4	46.3
	1993	100.0	16.6	3.3	3.7	8.6	6.7	3.0	58.1
Canada	1992	100.0	13.1		3.6	7.3	3.6	1.5	70.8
	1993	100.0	22.5	0.9	4.5	15.6	6.0	1.5	49.0
Sweden	1992	100.0	8.9	2.2	4.4	6.7	3.3	1.1	73.3
	1993	100.0	18.6		6.5	7.8	8.5	3.6	55.1
United Kingdom	1992	100.0	10.8	2.7	5.4	10.8			70.3
	1993	100.0	15.4			23.0	3.8	7.7	50.1
Italy	1992	100.0	5.3			5.3			89.5
	1993	100.0	10.5		5.2	10.5			73.8

Table 3 (Continued)

Spain								
1992	100.0	5.0		0.8		1.7	0.8	91.6
1993	100.0	13.7	4.5			4.5	4.5	72.8
France								
1992	100.0							100.0
1993	100.0	11.1		11.1	16.7		5.5	55.6
Other countries								
1992	100.0	12.9	0.7	2.7	4.8	3.4	4.1	71.4
1993	100.0	17.8	1.4	4.6	8.9	3.9	1.8	61.6

Notes: calculated from the data of Table 1, Annex.

TABLE 4. DYNAMICS OF EMIGRATION FROM RUSSIA ACCORDING TO SECTORS AND REGIONS (PERSONS)

Regions	Total adult workable citizens	Sectors						
		Industry, energetics, transport, communications, material supply, construction	Agriculture, forestry, procurement	Trade, public catering, lodging and communal services insurance, management	Science and public education	Public health, social care, sport	Culture and arts	Other activities
Total:								
1992	58730	16164	8736	4623	4572	4110	1053	19472
1993	67775	19668	9813	4765	5876	4180	1135	22841
Mos-cow								
1992	10296	7	0	0	2	3	2	10296
1993	7891	589	8	152	436	250	120	6336
Omsk oblast								
1992	6043	1638	1914	779	543	363	115	691
1993	8243	3182	1796	875	760	359	64	1207
Altai region								
1992	5487	1001	2554	330	787	251	85	479
1993	5952	1064	2706	477	580	301	82	742

Table 4 (Continued)

Moscow oblast								
1992	913	558	12	60	108	97	87	41
1993	898	313	17	51	160	141	87	129
Chelyabinsk oblast								
1992	3179	730	47	188	146	677	62	145
1993	1555	695	30	95	194	501	4	36
Leningrad oblast								
1992	4679	1899	0	378	552	631	153	1066
1993	6081	1519	32	364	816	468	189	2693
Novosibirsk oblast								
1992	2169	720	20	134	23	169	8	433
1993	2001	633	395	116	249	199	35	374
Sverdlovsk oblast								
1992	1331	611	24	92	122	156	28	481
1993	2756	797	15	89	155	134	47	1519
Volgograd oblast								
1992	1514	640	514	120	69	86	9	731
1993	3127	942	841	77	136	113	6	1012
Krasnodar region								
1992	1995	681	225	290	72	135	15	155
1993	2127	1074	22	296	189	172	25	151
Kemerovo oblast								
1992	2084	694	79	149	147	105	19	138
1993	2197	1070	68	124	228	126	13	568

Table 4 (Continued)

	Year								
Orenburg oblast	1992	1954	1954	680	1165	185	137	25	803
	1993	3228	611	791	216	220	123	26	1241
Saratov oblast	1992	794	340	512	40	11	52	25	53
	1993	2215	470	804	96	139	132	16	558
Rostov oblast	1992	881	354	141	137	77	84	30	58
	1993	619	294	90	40	93	76	12	14
Tyumen' oblast'	1992	913	387	44	52	50	54	25	215
	1993	1002	428	38	71	67	37	32	329
Stavropol region	1992	627	244	22	106	82	78	18	244
	1993	979	129	26	34	74	78	18	620
Tomsk oblast'	1992	827	345	74	42	51	19	10	89
	1993	772	334	93	77	66	41	0	161
Cabardino Balkar republic	1992	962	449	140	165	90	37	10	71
	1993	1582	439	506	167	69	45	39	317
Others	1992	7779	2454	854	749	837	725	246	1914
	1993	15051	5085	1335	1348	1245	884	320	4834

TABLE 5. DISTRIBUTION OF EMIGRANTS FROM RUSSIAN FEDERATION
ACCORDING TO HOST (RECIPIENT) COUNTRIES AND ETHNIC GROUPS (PERSONS), 1992, 2-ND HALF

		Total number of emigrants						
		Germany	Israel	USA	Greece	Australia	Bulgaria	Hungary
Total no. of emigrants	48980	32438	8461	5449	656	370	201	37
Incl								
Russians	10645	5084	2392	1848	115	176	133	32
Ukrainians	860	445	138	191	10	7	11	1
Armenians	255	30	41	137	20	6	1	1
Jews	9734	936	5377	3066		144	6	1
Greeks	507	14	2	3	487			
Germans	25540	25469	13	24	1			
Not specified their ethnic origin	114	60	23	13	3		1	
Other ethnic groups	1325	400	475	167	20	37	49	2

TABLE 5 (CONTINUED)

Canada	Poland	Finland	France	Czechosloakia	Sweden	Other countries	Non-specified
156	108	181	27	61	81	394	360
94	79	132	19	44	78	257	162
2	4	11		4		22	14
5	1	2	1	1		5	4
46	3		4	6	3	12	130
							1
4			1			1	28
	3	2				4	4
5	18	34	2	6		93	17

Source: data from RF State Committee Statistics

TABLE 6. DISTRIBUTION OF EMIGRANTS FROM RUSSIAN FEDERATION
ACCORDING TO RECIPIENT COUNTRIES AND PROFESSIONS (PERSONS), 1992, 2-ND HALF

		Total number of emigrants				
		Germany	Israel	USA	Greece	Australia
Total, persons emigrated abroad, 16 years old and over	7	22098	6881	4334	505	286
Include those having profession or other source of living						
scientists	367	67	136	116	2	21
professors, teachers, tutors	1701	1185	288	141	15	15
include higher school	73	17	28	17	5	4
economists accountants	756	571	107	50	5	4
medical personnel	1176	600	317	173	22	15
engineers and technicians	1932	736	596	467	12	45
managers of enterprises, organization cooperatives	715	423	148	96	11	11
workers of all professions	11058	9541	815	387	151	13
students of higher school and colleges	839	347	260	146	15	14
retired persons, disabled, housewives	7680	4125	1978	1337	28	59
non-working	4717	1883	1284	939	152	55
other occupations	3182	1951	634	361	52	26
persons not specified their occupations	1215	669	318	121	40	8

Table 6 (Continued)

Bulgaria	Hungary	Canada	Poland	Finland
148	31	108	85	137
1	1	7	1	1
12	1	5	9	2
1			1	
3	2	2		2
5	1	5	1	9
4		14	5	9
2		5	1	2
15	1	7	15	17
9	1		6	3
12	1	5	2	8
50	18	40	31	59
19	3	11	8	21
16	2	17	6	4

Source: data from RF State Committee Statistics

TABLE 7. NUMBER OF SCIENTISTS FROM THE RUSSIA ACADEMY OF SCIENCES WENT ABROAD ON LONG-TERM (OVER 6 MONTH) CONTRACTS OUTSIDE THE AGREEMENTS WITH FOREIGN ACADEMIES OF SCIENCES AND OTHER ORGANIZATIONS

	1985	1986	1987	1988	1989	1990	1991	Total
USA	0	2	6	8	85	165	221	487
FRG	11	5	14	22	55	87	90	284
France	0	0	2	4	10	37	40	93
United Kingdom	0	2	5	4	9	13	35	68
Canada	0	0	4	2	5	8	25	44
Italy	0	1	0	3	2	12	21	39
Japan	2	1	2	1	4	7	19	36
Total	13	11	33	44	170	329	451	1051

Source: "Brain Drain" from Russia: Problems, Prospects, Ways, Regulation. Report to UNESCO-ROSTE seminar, February 21-24, 1994, Moscow, p.84.

Subject Index